Studies in German Literature, Linguistics, and Culture:
Literary Criticism in Perspective

About *Literary Criticism in Perspective*

Books in the series *Literary Criticism in Perspective*, a subseries of *Studies in German Literature, Linguistics, and Culture and of Studies in English and American Literature, Linguistics, and Culture*, trace literary scholarship and criticism on major and neglected writers alike, or on a single major work, a group of writers, a literary school or movement. In so doing the authors — authorities on the topic in question who are also well-versed in the principles and history of literary criticism — address a readership consisting of scholars, students of literature at the graduate and undergraduate level, and the general reader. One of the primary purposes of the series is to illuminate the nature of literary criticism itself, to gauge the influence of social and historic currents on aesthetic judgments once thought objective and normative.

Wolfgang Hildesheimer and His Critics

Patricia H. Stanley

Wolfgang Hildesheimer and His Critics

CAMDEN HOUSE

Copyright © 1993 by
CAMDEN HOUSE, INC.

Published by Camden House, Inc.
Drawer 2025
Columbia, SC 29202 USA

Printed on acid-free paper.
Binding materials are chosen for strength and
durability.

ISBN:1-879751-45-3

Library of Congress Cataloging-in-Publication Data

Stanley, Patricia Haas.
    Wolfgang Hildesheimer and his critics / Patricia H. Stanley. --
1st ed.
        p.   cm. -- (Studies in German literature, linguistics, and culture)
    Includes bibliographical references and indexes.
    ISBN 1-879751-45-3 (alk. paper)
        1. Hildesheimer, Wolfgang. 1916-   --Criticism and interpretation.
I. Title.   II. Series: Studies in German literature, linguistics, and culture
(unnumbered)
PT2617.I354Z95   1000012626
838'.91409--dc20
                                                                93-8417
                                                                CIP

Acknowledgments

I wish to thank Volker Jehle for his bibliographical assistance. I could not have examined a number of the texts cited here without his friendly cooperation. I am grateful, also, for the prompt editorial commentary of Eitel Timm and James Hardin. For his skill in technical matters I am indebted to Douglas Fisher, who responded to each of my queries with an unvarying patience, the competence of a computer expert, and the willingness to be of assistance that marks the true friend.

To the memory of Wolfgang Hildesheimer.

Contents

Introduction   xi

1: Narrative Fiction   1
    A. *Lieblose Legenden*   1
    B. *Paradies der falschen Vögel*   10

2: Reflective Texts   14
    A. *Vergebliche Aufzeichnungen*   14
    B. *Tynset*   18
    C. *Masante*   31
    D. Poetry   44

3: Nonfictional Texts   45
    A. *Zeiten in Cornwall*   45
    B. *Mozart*   52
    C. *Marbot*   62
    D. *Mitteilungen an Max über den Stand der Dinge und anderes*   74
    E. *Nachlese*   77

4: Dramas   79
    A. Hörspiele   80
    B. Stage Plays   87
    C. Television Plays   105
    D. Adaptations   105

5: Essays   107

6: Translations   112
  A. Narrative Fiction 112
  B. Plays   113

Conclusion   115

Works Consulted   118

Index   136

Introduction

WOLFGANG HILDESHEIMER, A PAINTER and graphic artist in Germany, began his writing career in 1950. In the following decade he published a collection of short stories, a novel, and several radio plays, most of which he also adapted for the stage. The dry, cosmopolitan wit of his stories soon gained him a reputation as a satirist; theater critics, on the other hand, regarded him as a dramatist of the absurd. Hildesheimer furthered this latter designation with university lectures and the publication, between 1959 and 1967, of a series of essays that describe his understanding of the absurd. These writings constitute the only theoretical discussion of the genre in German literary history, and although some critics refuse to accept Hildesheimer himself as an absurdist, his essays remain unchallenged.

With the publication in 1965 of his reflective book *Tynset* his fame spread throughout Europe and Asia, for the book was translated and acclaimed even in Japan. Hildesheimer did not become well known in English-speaking countries until 1981, with the translation of his controversial biography of Mozart (1977). His last major work, *Marbot* (1981), appeared in an English translation in 1983. This biography of a nineteenth-century English nobleman who never lived has attracted the attention, among others, of narratologists on both sides of the Atlantic. It should conclusively establish Hildesheimer as a writer of world literature, for other aspects of the text bear comparison with Vladimir Nabokov's fictive biography *Pale Fire* (1962), as well as Susan Sontag's *The Volcano Lover* (1992), Christa Wolf's *Kein Ort. Nirgends* (1981; translated as *No Place on Earth*, 1982), and, more obviously, Thomas Mann's *Doktor Faustus* (1947). The publication in 1987 of *The Collected Stories of Wolfgang Hildesheimer*, translated by Joachim Neugroschel, gives critics who do not read German all the more opportunity to examine the writer's worldview and his special interest in the arts.

Hildesheimer had begun to draw and create collages again in 1957 after moving to Switzerland, where he lived until his death on 21 August 1991. Some of his surrealistic pen-and-ink images appear in the reflective text *Vergebliche Aufzeichnungen* (Vain Sketches, 1962), the autobiographical *Zeiten in Cornwall* (Times in Cornwall, 1971), and the humorous-satirical *Mitteilungen an Max über den Stand der Dinge und anderes* ("Missives to Max," 1983) (which appears in translation in the Neugroschel book).

In 1973 and again in 1984 Hildesheimer announced that he was done with writing and was returning to his art career. His writing since 1973 is, indeed, markedly different from what preceded it, and he did create and exhibit significantly more collages; but he did not stop writing, even after 1984.

Hildesheimer is not the only writer in contemporary German literature with artistic ability. Günter Grass has illustrated his books; Peter Weiss and Christoph Meckel have exhibited their artwork; Hermann Hesse painted for pleasure; and Franz Kafka's pen-and-ink figures sometimes illustrate editions of his works. Hildesheimer is, however, unusual in that he expressed a preference for, and turned increasingly to, visual art as a creative medium.

For some time Hildesheimer had voiced the belief that scientific advances cause irreparable damage to the environment. He cited the destruction of trees in the Black Forest from factory and automobile emissions as one instance of this damage. Those in authority, however, refuse to do anything to halt or reduce pollution of air. As a result of this and other instances of environmental carelessness we live in an "Endzeit" (end time), a period that will mark the end of civilization as we know it. Hildesheimer's decision to eschew fiction writing and concentrate on art was motivated, he said in interviews, partly by a belief that fiction will not be read in the future – everyone will be too busy worrying about survival – and partly because of the pleasure he derived from creating art, particularly collages. The emphasis of his writing after 1973 shifted from first-person narratives to biographical texts and critical essays. After 1984 he wrote only essays on environmental issues and his main intellectual interests: art, music, and literature.

Substantial scholarly interpretations of Hildesheimer's work, including doctoral dissertations in America and Germany, began to appear in 1975. Early critics of the prose narratives written up to 1973 frequently insisted on identifying the first-person narrator with the author. They labeled the texts autobiography or exile literature or, conversely, literature of the absurd. Discussions of the plays centered on whether or not they were absurd.

More recent critics, especially in the period from 1985 to 1990, favor poststructuralistic, narratological, and phenomenological approaches to the various discourses. Debate continues about whether or not Hildesheimer is a writer of the absurd. The most unusual contribution to the controversy is Volker Jehle's *Werkgeschichte* (History of the Works, 1990), a comprehensive, uniquely personal, biographical, quasi interpretive, study. This weighty text includes chapters on Hildesheimer's work as a translator and graphic artist, aspects of his career that have been almost entirely ignored by researchers.

The definitive edition of Hildesheimer's oeuvre was published in September 1991 by Suhrkamp Verlag. It brings together the well-known texts and a large number of short pieces previously in limited circulation, including art criticism and essays on the environment and the arts. Unfortunately, the editors decided not to include any of Hildesheimer's translations or adaptations of British and Italian drama (all of which are listed in the present book under *Works Consulted*). Except for the short translation in the essay "Übersetzung und Interpretation einer Passage aus 'Finnegans Wake' von James Joyce" (Translation and Interpretation of a Passage from *Finnegan's Wake* by James Joyce), the *Gesammelte Werke* (Collected Works) gives no evidence of the writer's skill in translating or adapting texts.

The present evaluative study offers many suggestions for future research, and one of them is readily apparent from the above. The chapter "Hildesheimers Übersetzungen und Bearbeitungen" (Hildesheimer's Translations and Adaptations) in Jehle's book is not the final word on Hildesheimer as a translator. As rich as it is in biographical details and commentary, it should also serve as a valuable incentive for more objective readings of this aspect of the writer's oeuvre.

Jehle's chapter "Hildesheimer und die bildende Kunst" (Hildesheimer and Graphic Art) is a useful adjunct to several collections of collages: *Gedichte und Collagen* (Poetry and Collages, 1984); *Endlich Allein* (Finally Alone, 1985); *In Erwartung der Nacht* (Awaiting the Night, 1987); and *Landschaft mit Phoenix*, (Landscape with Phoenix) published posthumously in 1992. The artist included introductory essays in the 1985, 1987, and 1992 publications. Even though the original collages are unobtainable (for they are mainly in private collections), there may be enough material for a critical study of the writer as artist in the images that have been published, the artist's comments, the Jehle chapter, several essays included in the "Materialienbuch" *Wolfgang Hildesheimer* edited by Jehle in 1989, and the brief essay by Peter Horst Neumann, "Hildesheimer als bildender Künstler" (Hildesheimer as Graphic Artist), which contains a description of the collages as "Kunst als Recycling, ein herrliches Spiel, weit weg von den Worten" (Art as recycling, a splendid game far removed from words, 1991, 23).

The present text appears within the series Literary Criticism in Perspective, and shares the series' goal of providing a chronological discussion and evaluation of the criticism surrounding a specific writer in light of the social and historical influences of the time. To help depict the social climate in Germany, and as a general indicator of Hildesheimer's appeal to the public throughout his career, I include summaries of contemporary newspaper and magazine reviews of the plays and longer texts. Evaluative statements relate to the journal essays and book-length studies that began to appear after 1966, when Hildesheimer received two prestigious literary awards for *Tynset*. Among the critics whose judgments are discussed here are writers well known for their own creative and scholarly publications and doctoral candidates in the United States and Europe.

My specific goal is to provide a comprehensive evaluation of scholarship on Hildesheimer's writings and to offer suggestions for poststructuralistic-postmodernistic readings of his work. My aim is to point the reader away from the biographical impulse that figured so prominently in Hildesheimer research before 1980 and relegated this writer to a too narrow frame of reference. The appearance of *Marbot* in 1983 necessitates the expansive view that is advocated here.

Hildesheimer's *Gesammelte Werke* is the source for most citations in the following chapters, but quotations from *Das Ende der Fiktionen* (The End of Fictions) and the most familiar books (*Tynset, Masante, Mozart,* and *Marbot*) are cross-referenced to the individual editions listed under *Works Consulted*.

1: Narrative Fiction

A. *Lieblose Legenden*

HILDESHEIMER BEGAN HIS LITERARY career with a short story, "Der Kammerjäger" (The Sanitizer), which was published in March 1950 in the newspaper *Süddeutsche Zeitung*. He wrote many stories that year and the next. In 1952 twenty-two of them (but not the first one) were published under the title *Lieblose Legenden* (Loveless Legends). Modified versions of the collection were published over the years, and in 1982 the Suhrkamp publishing house brought out a special edition of the twenty-six stories that have appeared in the collection at one time or another.

Following the publication of the first edition of *Lieblose Legenden*, Adriaan Morriën described its stories as amusing, satirical parables, and he applauded Hildesheimer's dry Anglo-Saxon humor (1971, 85). This review points out two features that distinguish Hildesheimer from other German writers beginning their careers after World War II. First, Morriën calls attention to the British influence on Hildesheimer's literary voice. As an adolescent and as a young man Hildesheimer attended British schools. For two years (1940 to 1942) he taught English in Tel Aviv before he became a Public Information Officer for the British government in Jerusalem. As a simultaneous translator at the Nuremberg War Crimes Trials from 1946 to 1948[1] he continued to develop his ability to communicate in English. His dry wit in his native tongue is no doubt affected by this background. Second, Morriën, a Dutch reviewer, notes that humor and amusing parables are a welcome change from the resoundingly serious literature written in Germany shortly after World War II, especially among other members of Gruppe 47, the literary group formed in 1947 by Hans Werner Richter. German reviewers, too, mention the humor in *Lieblose Legenden*, but only Morriën specifically identifies its understated quality as British-inspired. He is one of the few who reacted with pleasure to its appearance.

All reviews that appeared soon after the book's publication are superficial, using but not explaining such terms as *satirical,*

---

[1] See Volker Jehle, *Wolfgang Hildesheimer* (Frankfurt am Main: Suhrkamp, 1989), 375-77 for a chronology of Hildesheimer's life to 1989.

ironical, parodistic, grotesque (Krolow 1989, 156), and *Kafkaesque*
(Jens 1971b, 81-82). Written primarily for newspapers and
magazines, these reviews offer general and generally similar im-
pressions.[2] Friedrich Sieburg, then the most influential literary
critic in the press, was wholeheartedly opposed to the abstract type
of social criticism produced by writers in Gruppe 47. Although
Sieburg himself did not review *Lieblose Legenden*, it might be that
the stories fell victim to an attitude similar to Sieburg's "blanket
condemnation" of the group's writing (Zimmermann 1988, 397,
392). The brief, impressionistic reviews may be a result of the
critical climate at that time. (See Zimmermann 1988, 393-401, for an
overview of journalistic criticism in the 1950s.)

Ernst Nef, writing for a Swiss journal in 1975, points out the
cosmopolitanism of the 1952 edition of *Lieblose Legenden* by comparing Hildesheimer stories with French plays by Eugene Ionesco
and Samuel Beckett. As he notes thematic similarities between "Ich
finde mich zurecht" (translated as "I Orient Myself") and Ionesco's
The New Tenant, he reminds his readers that the Hildesheimer
story appeared several years before Ionesco's play was first
performed in Germany in 1957 (1975, 38). (It premiered on the
English stage in 1956.) Similarly, Burckhard Dücker reports that
Hildesheimer used motives and themes in the early stories that
were only later taken up by Ionesco, Beckett, Arthur Adamov, and
Jean Genet, who are considered the creators of literature of the
absurd (1976, 3).

Dücker's book, originally written as a dissertation at the University of Heidelberg, is the first scholarly examination of Hildesheimer as an absurdist. It is firmly grounded in German literary
history and philosophy, and it takes a sociological approach to the
prose and plays through 1974. With the exception of the above reference to French writers and a discussion of French Surrealism as a
forerunner of the absurd (16-20), Dücker limits his comments to
German writers and theorists. His brief examination of *Lieblose
Legenden* emphasizes the conflict between an intellectual individual and society (43-50).

In his evaluative study of Hildesheimer's works to 1977 Heinz
Puknus devotes several pages to *Lieblose Legenden* and elaborates
on earlier references to the Kafkaesque quality of Hildesheimer's
parables and satires. His major contribution, however, is his realization that "Ich trage eine Eule nach Athen"(translated as "I Carry
an Owl to Athens"), "Der Brei auf unserem Herd" (translated as
"The Gruel On Our Stove"), and "Schläferung" (translated as

---

[2] See Volker Jehle, *Wolfgang Hildesheimer: Eine Bibliographie* (1984), 216-19 for
a listing of review articles.

"Sleep"), stories composed for the 1962 edition of the collection, are more sophisticated than the others. In "Schläferung," in fact, Puknus sees a pervasive melancholy lyricism that indicates to him the end of Hildesheimer's satirical phase (1978, 24-25).

Björn Andersson selects only a few stories in *Lieblose Legenden* to illustrate the development of alienation in Hildesheimer's absurd worldview. His 1979 book begins with a discussion of the concept of the absurd that relies heavily on French contributions to the genre. He then describes how Hildesheimer's basic premise differs from that of Albert Camus (see Chapter 4 below for additional discussion). Taken together, the Dücker and Andersson introductory chapters are far more useful than the references to Hildesheimer as a playwright in Martin Esslin's *Theatre of the Absurd* (1969), a popular primer on the genre but hardly comprehensive. Although the Esslin text has been revised several times, the entry for Hildesheimer remains the same in all editions.

In Andersson's opinion, Hildesheimer's literary alienation has a tripartite structure: the problematical figure, the world around this figure, and the ensuing conflict when the figure confronts the world. The artist in "Das Atelierfest" (translated as "The Studio Party") is representative of the outsider, the problematical figure, who cannot adapt to the society to which he seemingly belongs unless he makes unacceptable sacrifices. He can find no acceptable answer to the question of how he is to relate to his milieu, which consists of acquaintances who gather in his apartment and make merry just as he is about to begin a new painting.

The world in which this figure lives is well ordered and highly functional. The individual, who is subordinate to this order, is to suppress any protest he may have and maintain the order, which in "Atelierfest" means to join in the merrymaking. But order is only a semblance of order, and the individual is no individual at all, just a patchwork of various models (47-50). "Ich finde mich zurecht" offers an especially good example of the world, with its emphasis on the material things that ultimately decide how one is to live. Andersson notes a strong resemblance to Ionesco's play *Le nouveau locataire* (54-56), but he does not mention that the Hildesheimer story, published in the 1952 edition of *Lieblose Legenden*, precedes the play by several years. It is surely coincidental that both writers portray the world as dehumanized by things, for there is no evidence that Ionesco knew of Hildesheimer's work.

The dilemma of life for Hildesheimer's disillusioned outsider narrators is solved in "Warum ich mich in eine Nachtigall verwandelt habe" (translated as "Why I Changed Into a Nightingale") by the extraordinary metamorphosis that occurs, but the narrator's transformation is less striking than his belief that happiness is unattainable for a human. As a bird he can lead a pure and happy existence; that is, he need no longer wish or worry (153).

The Romantic poet Friedrich Hölderlin also extolled the carefree life of the nightingale in the fragment, "Und wenig wissen" (And few know), which contains the following lines: "Daß ich, wie Nachtigallen, ein sorglos Lied/Von meiner Wonne sänge!" ([That I, like nightingales, would sing a carefree song of my bliss!] Hölderlin 1961, 111). Hildesheimer's familiarity with this poet's work is clearly demonstrated in the course of *Mitteilungen an Max über den Stand der Dinge und anderes* (1983; see Chapter 3 below). To find a reference to Hölderlin as early as the 1952 edition of *Lieblose Legenden* suggests that Hildesheimer's literary beginning is not as uncomplicated as Puknus claims (1978, 25).

Andersson's book has a detailed table of contents that identifies the primary texts featured in each of its twenty-five sections. Unfortunately, the table is not consistently helpful. It does not show, for example, that the "Nachtigall" story is the central issue of Section 21.1 (149-53).

Nef, Dücker, and Andersson in the 1970s examined *Lieblose Legenden* more closely than Puknus and without biographical interpolations, but more noteworthy readings appeared in the 1980s in articles by Roderick Watt (1983) and Klaus Reichert (1987) and in Peter Hanenberg's *Geschichte im Werk Wolfgang Hildesheimers* (History in the Work of Wolfgang Hildesheimer, 1989); a structuralistic study of the phenomenon of melancholy in Hildesheimer's prose by Dietmar Goll-Bickmann (1989); and Jehle's biographical-interpretive *Werkgeschichte* (1990).

Goll-Bickmann focuses mainly on the reflective texts, but he devotes Part 2 of his six-part study to aspects of melancholy in the early stories (62-116). He defines literary melancholy as a phenomenon of the conscious mind that may be discovered in literature from the middle of the eighteenth century to the present. Unlike its pathological forms, literary melancholy always appears as both a therapeutic expression of sadness and a creative discharge of poetically productive energy (54-55). Goll-Bickmann summarizes several stories in *Lieblose Legenden* to explain why the majority of the narrators are not melancholics (62-88). Those narrators who do display characteristics of literary melancholy include the extremely sensitive, weak, and passive painter in "Das Atelierfest" and the equally weak and passive narrator of "Ich finde mich zurecht," who shows signs of clinical melancholia by the end of the story (92-97). With one exception, melancholy in *Lieblose Legenden* is a mood and not the phenomenon that interests Goll-Bickmann.

The exception is "Schläferung," whose first-person narrator is a fully-drawn melancholic and the forerunner of Hildesheimer's later narrators. Weary as he is of the world, he displays energy and certainty of purpose in his withdrawal from life. He is neither passive nor weak and expresses his melancholy in full consciousness of his distress. His is an aesthetic, productive act of consciousness with a utopian-reflective quality (112-13).

It is Goll-Bickmann's aim to clear away the confusion surrounding the term *melancholy* in Hildesheimer criticism. In Part 1 he summarizes the various critical texts that describe Hildesheimer's narrators or the writer himself as melancholy, and his research will certainly be useful for other scholars. He is partial, however, to serpentine sentences replete with dashes, colons, and lengthy quotations, and he requires a patient reader. Section 3.3 of Part 2, the discussion of "Schläferung," is relatively free from these stylistic peculiarities and reveals Goll-Bickmann's ability as a literary critic. His interpretation of the narrator's behavior as regressive, for example, is valuable.

Both Goll-Bickmann and Hanenberg refer to the Reichert essay. For Goll-Bickmann, Reichert is merely one of those critics who are intent on comparing the melancholy of Hildesheimer's narrators with Shakespearean models (Reichert 1987, 2). Hanenberg, however, expands on Reichert's insight that the sense of the uncanny in Hildesheimer's stories is related to historical events of the recent past and may be an expression of repressed feelings (Hanenberg 1989, 12).

Reichert also suggests that the author might not be aware that when he depicts the uncanny as the norm, he is influenced by the recent past. This notion of an unconscious aesthetic release of feelings takes on a good deal of significance when one considers the question of whether or not Hildesheimer is an absurdist, an issue that becomes important when we evaluate his dramatic works. Reichert offers even more useful material for further study in his conjecture that the term *allegory* may be a key to recognizing what Hildesheimer does in *Lieblose Legenden* and later fiction (1987, 78-81). (See Blamberger 1985, 76-77, for a passing reference to the stories in *Lieblose Legenden* as metafiction, that is, as parodies of parodies of the legend form, a notion that merits further consideration.)

Hanenberg is apparently influenced by New Historicism in critical theory of the 1970s. He substantiates his opinion that Hildesheimer means to indict post-World War II German society by pointing out historical and political references in a selected group of stories from the 1982 edition of *Lieblose Legenden* (12-23). (Hanenberg dates the edition 1983, one of the few typographical errors in his text.)

"Schläferung" appears in a separate section of Hanenberg's book as one of the "Texte der Trauer" (Texts of Sadness). He and Goll-Bickmann quote the same passage, in which the anonymous narrator refers to "Mörder und Schwachsinnigen" (murderers and retardates), and both agree that the reference is to recent history (Hanenberg 1989, 101; Goll-Bickmann 1989, 115). Hanenberg repeats the claim he made earlier that the narrators of *Lieblose Legenden* are retreating from the present, but the reader might not be convinced that "Schläferung" is grounded in the recent past. The reader might be just as likely to place the quoted words in the timelessness of this particular text within a Shakespearean context, as Reichert does (1987, 75).

Jehle, too, devotes a special section to "Schläferung," which was first printed in the 1962 edition of *Lieblose Legenden*. He describes the story as uniquely melancholy and reflective within the collection and suggests that it was included in the new edition for editorial reasons (1990, 68). Jehle's discussion is often more factual and biographical than interpretive, which highlights the special position he occupies in Hildesheimer research.

Jehle does not tell the reader of his privileged status as Hildesheimer's official archivist, but the fact that he held the position from 1982 to 1990 is well known in European literary and critical circles.[3] Because he had access to unpublished material and was in close contact with the writer during those years, Jehle can weave both factual and merely anecdotal details into his biographical, sometimes psychological, interpretation of Hildesheimer's writing and artwork. His *Werkgeschichte* is as unique in Hildesheimer scholarship as James Boswell's biography of Samuel Johnson, written two centuries earlier, and readers may feel that it is sometimes as invasive of Hildesheimer's privacy as Boswell's recording of private conversations with Johnson (see Clifford 1970, 119).

While Jehle does not reveal as many personal details as, for example, Diane Wood Middlebrook, who incorporates information from taped psychiatric sessions in her 1991 biography of the American writer Anne Sexton, he does exploit his personal knowledge of the writer in what is intended as a biographical history cum interpretation of Hildesheimer's oeuvre. The combination produces a singularly intimate portrait of the writer at work and interpretations of the works that are not always supported by the text in question. So far as *Lieblose Legenden* is concerned, however, Jehle helpfully identifies themes and images that will remain significant and gives us his definition of the Hildesheimer reader.

---

[3] The Hildesheimer-Archiv is presently housed at the Akademie der Künste, Archiv und Bibliothek, Hanseatenweg 10, D-1000 Berlin 21. The Archiv-Direktor is Dr. Wolfgang Trautwein.

The concept of truth as invention, first expressed in "Die Suche nach der Wahrheit" (The Search for Truth), for one example of a recurring theme, becomes the point of departure for several texts, including *Marbot* (1990, 12-14). "Der Brei auf unserem Herd" foreshadows a preoccupation with environmental pollution that will be expressed much more forcefully later. The narrator's retreat from society, presented most lyrically in "Schläferung," is a feature of every later text with the exception of *Zeiten in Cornwall* (58-75).

The narrator of "Die Suche nach der Wahrheit" is scornful of his readers, whom he regards as pragmatic, self-centered people who take no risks and uncritically accept whatever "truths" are told to them. The narrator himself knows that there are no truths, only probabilities and uncertainties. This same mocking narrator appears in all of the stories of the *Lieblose Legenden* except the lyrical "Schläferung," according to Jehle. He does not discuss all of the stories, only those he considers most important: "Die Suche nach der Wahrheit," "Der Riese" (The Giant), "Das Ende einer Welt" (The End of a World), "Ich trage eine Eule nach Athen," "Der Brei auf unserem Herd," and "Schläferung" (see 12-14, 14-18, 18-27, 51-58, 58-66, 66-75, respectively).

Roderick Watt concentrates on the implied reader of a Hildesheimer text and the effect of the narrator's mocking tone on the reader in his 1983 essay, which is also applicable to later texts. Hildesheimer's implied reader belongs to a group of highly educated but not necessarily highly cultured people "sometimes contemptuously referred to in German as the *Bildungsbürgertum*." This implied reader is also the person satirized in the stories. Because the reader is educated enough to appreciate the "consummate artistry" of the prose, however, this reader will dissociate him- or herself from its satirical purpose and thus "render ineffectual the intended satire" (62). Watt does not consider the possibility that the satire is intentionally undermined, but it is worth pondering as an early indication of the postmodern tendencies that Hildesheimer exploits so dramatically in *Marbot* (1981b).

Four narrative devices locate Hildesheimer's implied reader. The first is "casual asides ... which appeal to ... a certain kind of reader in the reading process" (63). The second device is based on the use of proper names, for Hildesheimer either implies (usually in an aside) that a fictional name should be familiar to the reader, or he combines fictional with genuinely historical names. The literate reader might well feel challenged to distinguish between the two "and thereby betray the very vice of name-dropping" that is being satirized (65). In addition, Hildesheimer uses genuine names "as a socially, educationally and culturally conditioned code" (66). To avoid a lengthy description of a Rococo atmosphere in "Das

Ende einer Welt," for example, he simply remarks that the scene reminds him of a painting by Watteau. Watt does not explain the satirical intent of this device, and indeed, when Hildesheimer makes use of the "code" in later narratives he intends no satire or criticism.

In the last two of the narrative devices that Watt identifies, Hildesheimer reveals that his implied reader is someone with "academic pretensions" (67). In addition to parodying "the turgid, pseudo-scientific jargon of many would-be-critics and scholars in the liberal arts" (68), he subtly imitates the style of famous texts (for example, Goethe's *Italienische Reise* [Italian Journey], 1817) that would be well known only to someone with an academic background. The stories most illustrative of these two parodic devices are: "Ich schreibe kein Buch über Kafka" (translated as "I Am Not Writing a Book on Kafka"), "1956 – ein Pilzjahr" (translated as "1956 – A Pilz Year"), "Bildnis eines Dichters" (translated as "Portrait of a Poet"), "Aus meinem Tagebuch" (translated as "From My Diary"), "Westcottes Glanz und Ende" (translated as "Westcotte's Rise and Fall"), and "Das Gastspiel des Versicherungsagenten" (translated as "The Insurance Agent's Guest Appearance"). Only an academic or someone in a profession related to higher education will understand the esoteric references and recognize the formal targets of this sharply pointed prose. Watt concludes that Hildesheimer "sacrifices satirical effect to literary virtuosity" (69). As a result, he attracts as readers only those whom he means to criticize. This virtuosity is an "obsession or at least a literary mannerism" (70).

It is certainly a hallmark of Hildesheimer's style that he (like Thomas Mann, with whom he is sometimes compared) addresses only a well-educated reader in all his texts, but the implied reader is not always a smug, superficial, name-dropping academic. In fact, the academic as implied reader is only a sometime target within the collection itself in its various editions. "Schläferung," the last story of the 1962 edition, has no satirical aim, as Watt notes. He is thus in agreement with Puknus (1978, 24-25) and with Jehle (1990, 68).

Jehle finds no satire in "Ich trage eine Eule nach Athen," first published separately in 1954, and "Der Brei auf unserem Herd," published for the first time in 1958. The narrator of these texts and "Schläferung," none of which Watt discusses, employs a confidential tone as he obliquely reveals his discomfiture in, and his plan (in "Schläferung") to retreat from, the world. The narrator expects the reader to understand the metaphorical structure of "Ich trage eine Eule nach Athen," and "Der Brei auf unserem Herd," as well as his references to Mona Lisa and Mary, Queen of Scots in

"Schläferung," but the narrative devices that will "pillory" the academic specialist, as Watt says (1983, 65), are no longer in evidence.

In 1990 Hildesheimer published a collection of very short pieces in a limited edition titled *Mit dem Bausch dem Bogen* (an idiomatic expression that resembles the American "a pig in a poke"). The ten satirical sketches or "Glossen," while never included in the *Lieblose Legenden*, were written in 1952, just after the first edition of *Lieblose Legenden* was published and are similar in style and tone. They appeared in the journal *Zeitschrift*, founded specifically for texts by Gruppe 47 members, which collapsed before the end of 1952 due to the generally poor quality of submissions. Volume 7 of the *Gesammelte Werke* (559-69) contains only four of the untitled "Glossen," numbered 1, 3, 6, and 9 in *Mit dem Bausch dem Bogen*. The seventh piece is especially interesting, however, for it foreshadows the *Tynset* narrator's intensely subjective, melancholy preoccupation with the visual and aural connotations of the letters in the word *Tynset*, especially the *y*. In this instance the word is *Ehe* (marriage), and in this early text the narrator projects confidence in his ability to solve the marital crisis that he cheerfully trivializes (1990, 24-26).

Mit dem Bausch dem Bogen, Lieblose Legenden in its 1982 edition, and Jehle's insights in *Werkgeschichte* will orient the reader to the range of Hildesheimer's themes and his technical idiosyncrasies. Just as the cultural and educational requirements for a Hildesheimer reader do not essentially change in later works, neither do Hildesheimer's preoccupations as a writer. Jehle's two-part examination of *Lieblose Legenden* (1990, 9-27, 47-75) is an invaluable research tool. He cross-references each theme and plot, includes little-known biographical information, and, with his reference to the French philosopher Montaigne (73-74), underscores the presence already evident early in the writer's career of a European, rather than postwar German, outlook. The "Glossen" of *Mit dem Bausch dem Bogen* furnish even more evidence of his cosmopolitanism and should be included in any study of Hildesheimer fiction.

Günter Blöcker, who was, with Sieburg, the most influential of the critics writing for the *Frankfurter Allgemeine Zeitung* in the 1950s and 1960s (Zimmermann 1988, 395), describes the Hildesheimer of *Lieblose Legenden* as a German Borges (not in a critique of that book but in a review of *Tynset*; 1965, 486). Critics of later and longer works find stylistic or thematic relationships between Hildesheimer and the French and British writers Albert Camus (Loquai 1986, 58), James Joyce (Koebner 1971, 55; Durzak 1976, 275), Samuel Beckett (Haas 1975, 95; Nef 1975, 38; Dücker 1976, 3;

Wohmann 1989, 204), Eugene Ionesco (Nef 38; Dücker 3), Oscar
Wilde (Hill 1976, 91), and Djuna Barnes (Jens 1971b, 122; Durzak
275; Wohmann 204). It would be worthwhile to locate these
relationships in the short stories and to develop Blöcker's reference
to the Argentinian writer Jorge Luis Borges (1899-1986), with its
intimation of a magical realism in the stories of *Lieblose Legenden*.
New readings that focus on the cosmopolitan framework of the
stories would effectively open them up to study by scholars in comparative literature, the context most suitable for them. Neugroschel's translation of many of the stories (1987) should be helpful.

Additional research, also, into the relationship between Hildesheimer and the French absurdists would expand our knowledge of
literature (and theater) of the absurd. *Lieblose Legenden*, the satirical "Glossen," and the essays on the absurd listed in Chapter 5
below would be the logical place to begin such a project. Although
it is in the plays that Hildesheimer more graphically exploits his
absurdist worldview, the short stories – which inspired some of the
plays – convey his message with equal effect and more subtlety.

A close reading of the stories of *Lieblose Legenden* that focuses
on intertextuality would help us to appreciate the longevity of Hildesheimer's concerns as a writer. A more thorough New Historicist
reading of the stories is needed, too, now that Hanenberg has made
a start in that direction. A final suggestion is to examine the
"author-function" in Hildesheimer's writing (see Foucault 1977).

B. *Paradies der falschen Vögel*

Anton Velhagen, the narrator of the novel, *Paradies der falschen
Vögel* (Paradise of the Rogues, 1953), employs the same dry and
elegantly witty tone that characterizes most stories of *Lieblose
Legenden*. Here, too, the narrator assumes that his reader is as
knowledgeable about art and music as he. Accordingly, he wastes
no time describing El Greco when he tells us about various paintings that his uncle, an art forger, created in an El Greco style and as-
cribed to an invented artist named Ayax Mazyrka. The difference
here is that the implied reader is not under satirical attack for pre-
tentious behavior, nor is the pedantic academic or the pragmatic
citizen a target. This implied reader is a confidant(e) of the narrator,
someone assumed to be as well educated as he and therefore un-
dismayed by allusive remarks sprinkled throughout the text. For
the most part they are not obscure, in any event: Beethoven, da
Vinci, even Carl Maria von Weber are well known. Robert
Guiscard, the alias appropriated from history by the narrator's

uncle, may be unfamiliar to some, but the implied reader is sure to own a selection of reference books and will be in the habit of using them. This reader is the implied reader of all Hildesheimer texts after *Lieblose Legenden*.

Early reviewers of *Paradies der falschen Vögel* describe it either as an ironic and amusing story (Süskind 1971, 86; Böll 1989, 165) or as the melancholy work of a moralist (Piontek 1989, 163; Wellershoff 1989, 162). Later critics remain unimpressed. Puknus does not take the novel seriously (1978, 25-26); Hanenberg merely devotes a few pages to historical references (1989, 29-33); Goll-Bickmann points out that Anton Velhagen conquers his melancholy moments by remembering pleasant events, for this narrator has no wish to be a Hamlet (1989, 100). Jehle notes particularities that appear in later works and biographical information (1990, 27-46). To date no one has undertaken a full-scale investigation of the novel that Walter Jens once eagerly awaited so that he might see how Hildesheimer would develop the dialectics at work in *Lieblose Legenden* (1971b, 83).

Oddly enough, in an interview conducted by Jens in 1971 Hildesheimer made a statement that might well have deterred critical study of the novel at a time when his works were being discovered by doctoral candidates in America and Europe. He told Jens that he would eliminate this text from his oeuvre if he could (1971a, 94), which implies that he regarded it as an unsuccessful effort. He contradicted himself in an interview some years later, however, declaring that the novel meant more to him than most of his plays; he did not explain why (Durzak 1976, 274).

When the novel first appeared in 1953 it was probably a victim of *Lieblose Legenden*. As pleased as the Dutch critic Morriën was to see humor return to the German literary scene (1971), German readers themselves preferred texts by other writers, among them Heinrich Böll and Wolfdietrich Schnurre, who made fewer demands on the general reader.[4] In 1953 as (then) West Germans were creating a *Wirtschaftswunder* (economic miracle), readers who had been unable to appreciate the esoteric satire and intertextual subtleties in *Lieblose Legenden* probably ignored the appearance of Hildesheimer's first novel, anticipating that it would be equally difficult to understand. There was no second edition of the book by Desch, which reprinted the original edition in 1967, no

---

[4] By 1979 61,000 copies of *Lieblose Legenden* had been printed, as compared with 490,000 copies of Heinrich Böll's collection of satirical stories, *Nicht nur zur Weihnachtszeit* (Not Only at Christmas), originally published in 1966. See Watt (1983, 72). Watt also quotes a comment made by Wolfdietrich Schnurre to the effect that satire cannot be too subtle, for it can only hope to influence the less sophisticated reader (69).

doubt to capitalize on the writer's fame as the recipient of two prestigious literature prizes in 1966 (for *Tynset*). A pocketbook edition was printed in 1959 by Goldmann Verlag, and the impetus at this time might have been Hildesheimer's fame as a dramatist of the absurd.

In 1953, however, he was relatively unknown, merely one of the numerous new writers of Gruppe 47, which he was invited to join in 1951. At that time Hans Werner Richter, the group's founder, welcomed Hildesheimer's witty, satirical, cosmopolitan stories as a refreshing change from "Kahlschlagprosa," the forceful but stylistically sterile prose (*kahl* = barren) that was preferred by writers of Gruppe 47 for exposing postwar attitudes (Richter 1986, 38). An early example, in fact the first story to be read at a Gruppe 47 meeting, is Schnurre's "Das Begräbnis" (The Burial), in which the advertised time and place of God's funeral attracts no one to the cemetery but the inspector of funerals and the narrator. Everyone else is presumably working in the brightly lit factory. The narrator describes his surroundings and records the gravediggers' fragmented slang remarks with an economy of words that matches the threadbare clothing of the workers (Schnurre 1969, 3-10). The reader confronts a setting where poverty of goods and spirit mingle. Hildesheimer also describes poverty of spirit, but his subtle, elegant prose and the milieu he portrays did not appeal to the general reader in Germany at that time.

Whatever he thought about his novel in 1971, Hildesheimer remained so interested in its convoluted plot in the 1950s that he based three plays and a short story on it. *Begegnung im Balkanexpress* (Chance Meeting in the Balkan Express), a radio play, was first broadcast in February 1953, almost simultaneously with publication of the book. The short story, "Aus meinem Tagebuch" (translated as "From My Diary"), was published separately in 1955 and included in the 1956 and later editions of *Lieblose Legenden*. The radio plays, *An den Ufern der Plotinitza* (On the Shores of the Plotinitza, 1954) and *Die Bartschedel-Idee* (Bartschedel's Idea, 1957), are also derivative.

It is unusual in any writer's career for one work to spawn so many variations; an objective explanation in this case might be simply that the *Paradies* plot contained intricacies that could be otherwise exploited. In each derivative text, however, just as in the novel itself, the narrator either falsifies his identity or circumstances falsify it for him, and he makes no real effort to rectify the error. According to Jehle, each narrator's desire for, or acceptance of, the anonymity afforded by falsification echoes the author's increasingly urgent wish to retreat from society because he was sorry he had decided to become a writer (1990, 40). In 1957, when

Hildesheimer began to paint again, he accomplished a retreat of sorts by moving to Poschiavo, a remote village in Switzerland. Retreat from society remained a Hildesheimer theme throughout his career and a personal goal even in Switzerland, where he was elected to honorary citizenship in 1983. When he worked on a collage in his studio, he said, he could forget the present and the approaching annihilation of the world as we know it (Lebert 1990).

Hildesheimer's well-known opinion that the novel in post-Nazi Germany is no longer a viable literary form was published in the essay "Die Wirklichkeit des Absurden" (The Reality of the Absurd) in 1967 (1991a, 7, 57-58). Once he also determined that he could only write from a personal perspective, as he stated in numerous interviews, it was obvious that he would not write a second novel. *Paradies der falschen Vögel* is thus our only example of how Hildesheimer would write novels if he had not come to the conclusion that they cannot adequately express reality. Since he was for a time so preoccupied with the plotline of the novel that he used variations of it in several other texts, it might be worthwhile to take a closer look at the society he portrays here and in the related narratives.

2: Reflective Texts

A. *Vergebliche Aufzeichnungen*

BETWEEN 1953 AND 1962 Hildesheimer wrote more than twenty original plays for stage, radio, and television, in addition to adaptations and translations. In 1957 he began to devote more time to art, as well. *Vergebliche Aufzeichnungen* (Vain Sketches), which appeared originally in the newspaper *Die Zeit* in 1962 and in book form the following year, contains seven surrealistic pen-and-ink drawings from this period. For the 1989 edition he replaced the drawings with collages that feature printed matter. In two instances an artful arrangement of letters spells nothing; in the other collages Hildesheimer uses phrases from his text, an Italian quotation, and a line from the Rilke poem, "Herbsttag" (Autumn Day). These images may constitute a subtext, but no one has yet investigated the possibility.

The monologist of *Vergebliche Aufzeichnungen* begins and ends his reflections with the confession that he can think of nothing to write: everything is old, has already happened or been written about, or both. Hans F. Nöhbauer, who reviewed the work in 1963 for the "Book of the Week" column of a Munich newspaper, compares Hildesheimer's book to Hugo von Hofmannsthal's "Lord Chandos Brief" (Lord Chandos Letter) at the turn of the century. In this fictional letter the writer complains of his inability to think or speak coherently about anything, but he states his complaint eloquently and thereby proves how coherent he can be. Hildesheimer's monologue reveals a similar language crisis and its conquest.

Thomas Koebner, who writes from a Marxist perspective about Hildesheimer's intellectual heroes, describes the narrator as alienated and deeply pessimistic but still searching for something new to say about history or personal deeds. The mythic sameness of the ocean is a metaphor for the negative, unchanging facade of a world where no fantasy is allowed to survive. In such a setting the narrator is a literary mirror image of the melancholy Hamlet, since both men continually search for a reason to act but cannot bring themselves to do anything. Alienation is a condition of, but at the same time an impediment to, life for Hildesheimer's heroes (1971, 44-45).

Dücker contradicts Nöhbauer and modifies Koebner's Marxist point of view when he says that the text is not concerned with language but with the institution of literature itself and the absurd orientation of numerous writers in post-Hitler Germany. The imprint of history so permeates the "Stoff" (substance) of which literature is made, that this "Stoff" is no longer amenable to creative possibilities. To thematize the self is the only recourse for these writers (1976, 71).

Solipsism is the term Puknus chooses to describe the narrator's attitude. *Vergebliche Aufzeichnungen* formally introduces a new phase in Hildesheimer's career in which a radically introverted and melancholy "I" focuses on itself. In this first of several solipsistic narratives of the 1960s the "I" searches a beach for the last time, hoping to find something he can write about; but he rejects everything he finds, including a skull, as already exhausted of interest. The narrator accepts finding nothing to write about as an invitation or compulsion to remain silent, if only for the time being (1978, 68-69). With this interpretation, a reader should not pity the narrator (Lenz 1989, 190) but admire his ability to rationalize a situation feared by most writers more than rejection of a manuscript.

Of course, *Vergebliche Aufzeichnungen* is more than a case history of writer's block. Andersson (1979), Günter Blamberger (1985), and Goll-Bickmann (1989) direct their attention to what is positive in the text, and they find existential meaning. According to Andersson, the narrator – who seeks order in his life – creates order (albeit of a negative cast) as he determines that everything has indeed been done or written (122). Blamberger says that the search itself was not in vain, for the possibilities of understanding the meaning of the world have now been set aside as possibilities (82). Goll-Bickmann's structuralistic approach is a welcome response to the claims of a language-based crisis in the text. The narrator cannot find any new material on the beach, it is true; but as he reflects on the objects he sees he creates a new form of communication that strives for balance between the useful and the useless. This "Sprache der Melancholie" (language of melancholy) is a musical, subjective, didactic speech that requires a listener (reader) because it can be incomprehensible to the speaker himself (318), an insight that might be compared with Reichert's observation that Hildesheimer is perhaps unaware of influences from the recent past when he writes (1987, 67-81).

Goll-Bickmann does not explain why he considers the speech musical, but it might be because the tone of the discourse continually shifts from positive to negative, creating an oscillating, rhythmic motion of ideas. One can even impose a musical structure on what Goll-Bickmann describes as the threefold framework of the discourse. The threat of failure, a transitory sense of having found a solution, but at the end a sense of frustration again when the narrator says that he has found nothing (485, note 25) resemble the exposition, development, and recapitulation found in sonata form.

Hanenberg's thesis is that the monologist can find nothing to write about because, as he takes up objects on the beach – particularly the skull – and contemplates their possible histories, he realizes he can do nothing more than invent their beginnings – because reality intrudes for example, as soon as the narrator wonders whether the skull could be that of a Jew. Too much horror has happened in reality and been distorted by those who miswrite history for the narrator to be able to think of anything to say (1989, 90-94). He is silenced not by a creative block but by historical events.

In contrast to Hanenberg's poststructuralistic focus on the narrator's historical position and Goll-Bickmann's structuralistic orientation, Jehle reads the narrator's reflections biographically as evidence of a midlife crisis experienced by the author, the outcome of which is withdrawal from his literary career and a return to art. Jehle bases his interpretation on a passage in the text and, apparently, on personal knowledge. He claims that the paragraphs in which the narrator ponders the identity of the skull comprise a disguised self-portrait of Hildesheimer. When the narrator reflects that the jester spoke the truth, but no one at court understood him (Hildesheimer 1991a, 1, 293-96), the author wants to justify his earlier texts, which received what he considered derogatory reviews. (Early critics, for example, often read *Lieblose Legenden* as merely a collection of amusing anecdotes.) At the end of his reflections the monologist leaves the beach, and the writer renounces his literary career now that he has confirmed the senselessness of writing (Jehle 1990, 84-88).

There is a flaw in his interpretation that Jehle himself mentions but does not resolve: Hildesheimer did not give up his literary career. Only three years later he published *Tynset*, which many regard as his masterpiece. Jehle says merely that *Vergebliche Aufzeichnungen* gives the reader a false impression. The impression is false, of course, only if the reader confuses the first-person narrator with Hildesheimer and reads the text as an autobiography.

Another assertion should also be questioned. Jehle's claim that Hildesheimer's midlife crisis is reflected in the discourse of *Vergebliche Aufzeichnungen* contradicts to some extent a comment Hildesheimer made to Dierk Rodewald in a 1971 interview. Asked why he publicized his withdrawal from literature in the 1962 text, the writer replied that the narrator does not necessarily speak for him. He acknowledged that between twenty and eighty percent of what the narrator says is true for him, too, but it is not true that he "unbedingt und immer" (unconditionally and always) records his own thoughts and opinions in his work. The sketches

("Aufzeichnungen") are not a failure or vain attempt ("vergeblich"). They do not mean to suggest that writing is a senseless pursuit (Rodewald 1971b, 155).

Jehle, who offers no evidence to support what amounts to his rejection of the interview response, regards the sketches as confirmation of a personal failure so overwhelming that – even though there is no basis for this interpretation in the text – he thinks the narrator might have considered suicide (1990, 88). Since Jehle continually juxtaposes narrator and author, the reader might infer that Hildesheimer, too, thought about suicide as he wrote, and with this notion the objective value of the discourse is diminished. For example, the central image of *Vergebliche Aufzeichnungen* is the skull and its possible identity as that of a court jester. If the reader accepts Jehle's claim that the narrator's musings about the jester are a cloaked authorial rebuttal to past critical reviews, the monologue becomes so autobiographical that the reader might well overlook the historical and social references that Dücker and Hanenberg regard as significant, as well as the Goll-Bickmann identification of a new form of communication in this text.

Jehle's significant contribution in the present context is an explanation of the role played by Hamlet in Hildesheimer's literary life (85-86). Shakespeare's melancholy Dane incorporates the concepts of guilt and innocence that are explored only briefly in *Vergebliche Aufzeichnungen* but are central to *Tynset, Masante,* and the stage and radio plays. The author even began to write a Hamlet novel in 1961. What remains of his intention is a fragment, published as "Aus einem aufgegebenen Roman" (From a Discarded Novel) in a collection titled *Exerzitien mit Papst Johannes* (Catechisms with Pope John, 1979). It is listed as "Hamlet: Ein Fragment" in the *Gesammelte Werke* (1991a, 1, 259-72).

Hanenberg, who also comments on Hildesheimer's interest in Hamlet, adds that Shakespeare's character was a significant figure for other postwar writers, including Alfred Döblin, whose 1956 novel is titled *Hamlet oder Die lange Nacht nimmt ein Ende.* (Hamlet or The Long Night Comes to an End). Hildesheimer's narrator, much like Hamlet, is haunted by figures from the past. Like Hamlet, he holds a skull in his hand and ponders whose it might be. It is not that he cannot think of anything to say (he is not troubled by writer's block) but that the skull signifies so much that his thoughts come to a halt. He remembers the murder of Hamlet's father and the murders of Jews in the recent past. He remembers, too, how the latter murders have been explained away by the murderers themselves and by historians, and he can think of no course of action to take, no way to investigate the truth regarding these murders. Hanenberg's identification of the social criticism within this ostensibly personal text is an important contribution to Hildesheimer criticism and to post-1945 literature in general.

Suhrkamp Verlag republished this text early in 1989, and Hildesheimer gave a public reading from it soon afterward in Zurich. A Swiss reviewer commented that the author could be mistaken for a postmodernist (Meyer 1989), suggesting – even before the appearance of Hanenberg's book that same year – the openness of Hildesheimer's discourse.

B. *Tynset*

Hildesheimer's reputation as a serious writer was established with the publication of *Tynset* in early 1965. In 1966 he received two prestigious awards for this monologue, the Georg Büchner Prize and the Literature Prize of the City of Bremen. Reviews in Germany in the spring and summer of 1965 were mainly laudatory; Hans Schwab-Felisch, for example, describes Hildesheimer's prose as classical and his mastery of the alternately reflective and narrative styles admirable (197). Walter Jens also refers to the classical prose of *Tynset* and claims that this prose is richer in nuances than that of any German writer since Thomas Mann (1971c, 126). Roland H. Wiegenstein is impressed by the new form of monologue that Hildesheimer has chosen, which has none of the breathless quality of the interior monologue (1971, 129). Gabriele Wohmann, like Jens a well-known writer of fiction, uses the word *Perfektion* when she describes Hildesheimer's prose (1989, 204).

On the other hand, Peter Horst Neumann writes that the book could have been a masterpiece, but tactlessness mars its content. There is superfluous material and not enough mystery. Artistry is lacking in the descriptive passages that surround the word *Tynset*, and there is an unfortunate number of banal and platitudinous remarks. All these trivial errors should have been corrected by an editor (1989, 211). Reinhard Baumgart, in a similar vein, expresses his annoyance with clichés and banalities (1971, 115-18).

Hermann Kähler, writing in 1965 for the East German journal *Sinn und Form*, compares the "situation" in *Tynset* with two socialistic texts, Konstantin Simonov's play *Der Vierte* (The Fourth One) and Christa Wolf's novel *Der geteilte Himmel* (translated as *Divided Heaven*). The situation in the East German texts develops to resolution, but in *Tynset* it is circular and merely confirms that history repeats itself (793). The narrator's refusal to act against the presence of fascism in contemporary West Germany makes this a weak text, since it does not challenge the reader to take an active part in social reality. With respect to the circularity of the text, Kähler identifies a labyrinthine form of narration and a wavelike flow. The former occurs in episodes that describe the labyrinth of the Villa Barbarigo and the narrator's attempt to drive through a German city (Hildesheimer 1965c, 96-98, 111-22; see also Hildesheimer 1991a, 2, 58-59, 66-72), and the latter in the episodes of the concert of roosters and the summer bed (1965c, 63-70, 191-214; 1991a, 2, 40-43, 109-22).

Kähler finds nothing musical in Hildesheimer's book. In spite of textual references to its fugal form, he labels the summer bed episode a horrifying novella marked by an absurd orientation that the author has not yet been able to overcome. As a final weakness he notes that Hildesheimer was not able to separate himself from the narrator and create an independent figure (1965, 794-97). West German critics in the 1980s, especially those who focus on the historical significance of the book, frequently refer to Kähler's opinions.

The identity of the monologist was an important issue for most early reviewers. Hilde Domin (1965) and Helmut Heißenbüttel (1971) represent the objective view, Baumgart (1971) and Wiegenstein (1971) the subjective. Domin declares that it is not important whether the "I" is that of the author or an abstract narrator. This "I" is isolated from reality as if he were in a cage. All he has are his memories, which are "entsetzlich" (monstrously) well preserved. What he says in this sleepless night, even the abstruse, is valid for many, if not all, Germans (126). Heißenbüttel compares the narrator to the "Geist der Erzählung" (spirit of storytelling), who sets all the bells in Rome ringing at the beginning of Thomas Mann's 1951 novel *Der Erwählte* (translated as *The Holy Sinner*). Like this "spirit," the *Tynset* narrator is an amorphous, omnipresent being. Heißenbüttel describes him as a narrative construct of the grammatical "I" that is at the same time concrete. He shares some characteristics with the author, but he is a generalized figure (120-21). Baumgart, on the other hand, states unequivocally that the monologist is Hildesheimer himself (116), and many early reviews carry the same information. Perhaps the reviewers were influenced by the author, who concluded a 1965 magazine article "Antworten über Tynset" (Answers About Tynset) with the acknowledgment, "ich habe mehr von mir gesprochen als von dem Buch. Aber das ist eigentlich dasselbe" (I have said more about myself than about the book. But that is really the same thing; 1991a, 2, 387).

Wiegenstein's opinion that the narrator is half fictive and half autobiographical and that the author carefully chose whatever biographical information there is (129-30), begins, at least, to recognize that the narrator exists within a work of literature.

Scholarly studies of *Tynset* and of Hildesheimer's other works began to appear in 1975. With a few exceptions, these later critics concentrate on the content of the monologue rather than the identity of the monologist. The genre to which the book belongs becomes a matter of some dispute: several critics describe it as a novel, but others explain why it is not a novel. Since Hildesheimer said in "Antworten über Tynset" that he conceived of the text as the literary equivalent of a musical rondo (1991a, 2, 385), most critics at least mention the musical structure of the book. There are those, however, who regard the discourse as a stream of consciousness without structure, and for at least two critics the book's form is wavelike rather than musical.

Koebner, who traces the development of the narrator's alienation and melancholy mood in the prose up to 1970, describes *Tynset* as a stream-of-consciousness monologue that has such an unusual clarity that the narrator becomes a sentimental figure. He compares the book to an epistolary novel, for it is more open in its presentation of confessional material and experiences than, for example, Molly Bloom's famous monologue in *Ulysses* or that of Hans Schnier in Heinrich Böll's *Ansichten eines Clowns* (translated as *The Clown*; 1971, 55-56).

It is true that the narrator is more of a storyteller than Molly Bloom and probably more candid than Hans Schnier, but Patricia R. Haas does not consider him "open" in his confessions. The reader must often "rely on implication in order to develop the clues" the narrator gives us to his inner life (1975, 93).

Elizabeth Mayer Petuchowski explains that the anonymous narrator wants to escape from the world by finding a dwelling that holds no threats of persecution or memories. He expresses his desire in images of emptiness, which include not only actual empty places in the house but certain words (such as *no more* and *almost*) that convey emptiness, and objects – especially the telescope through which he seeks nothingness. This anonymous narrator belongs to the generation that witnessed Nazi persecution. He "experienced those years as persecuted Jew, as did his author" (1975, 6-7). The narrator is passive; his mood combines melancholy and resignation. Melancholy is "often associated with visual images of emptiness" in Hildesheimer's writing in general, and resignation is "linked with areas of emptiness where nothing happens" (13).

Petuchowski deals with the images of emptiness in *Tynset* and *Masante* as one manifestation of Hildesheimer's efforts to "come to terms with events which took place in Germany in recent times" (159). She concentrates on locating the images that demonstrate

melancholy but does not give us her definition of the term or mention Koebner's Marxist-oriented definition of melancholy as self-
analysis and the interior counterpart to satire, which analyzes
society (Koebner 1971, 37).

Goll-Bickmann refers to Petuchowski and Koebner in his structuralistic study of melancholy. Melancholy, he says, is to be understood as an artistic stance, for the narrator is not mentally ill.
Rather, his knowledge of the world and of himself makes it impossible for him to adapt to the prevailing social order. Misery, help-
lessness, tension, and conflict with one's conscience define the
term *Not* (misery), which Goll-Bickmann uses when he explains
the relationship between the signifying "I" and its signified misery
(1989, 212). He appropriates the term from Wolfgang Rath's 1985
semiotic study of a group of German novels, including *Tynset* and
Masante. Rath's opinions are generally too wide-ranging for Goll-
Bickmann, but he devotes considerable space to an examination of
Rath's linguistic analysis (1989, 126-43).

The most enlightening aspect of Goll-Bickmann's book is his
examination of the binary oppositions within the three dimensions of the narrator's guilt-innocence misery. The first dimension
is a conflict with respect to historical time, namely, the Nazi period
(248-61). The second and most complex dimension has to do with
the multiplicity and function of the godlike roles the narrator assumes (262-90). The third dimension is the narrator's ability to
compensate. For every bad or unpleasant image or event that he
describes, the narrator immediately juxtaposes a good one. His
reflections are thus a type of therapy, although he does not resolve
his melancholy. He lives and will continue to live on the border-
line between the poles of human existence, between a fleeting
moment of fulfillment and the threat of failure, between misery
and freedom from it, between what Goll-Bickmann calls a black
and a white melancholy (290-93).

The therapeutic value of the narrator's literary creativity is not a
new insight. Manfred Durzak refers to it in an essay that accompanies an interview with Hildesheimer in Durzak's large-scale
study of the German novel. This critic describes the narrator's
imaginative storytelling as a therapeutic response to his anxiety
and inner despair over his passivity and moral weakness in fleeing
from pursuers to a utopian nowhere. The storytelling is only infre-
quently successful as a compensatory device (1976, 303-4). Goll-
Bickmann, who does not mention Durzak's finding, emphasizes
the narrator's awareness of the problematical ambivalence of his
compensatory structure. It is his choice to remain in a state of constant but extraordinarily productive tension between the misery of

remembering the past and the aesthetic pleasure he derives from making stories (1989, 291-93).

Many scholars bring *Masante* into their discussions of *Tynset*, because the 1973 monologue is something of a sequel to *Tynset*. The first lengthy study of the earlier book is "*Tynset*: An Analysis of Wolfgang Hildesheimer's Lyrical Modernism" (1975), by Patricia R. Haas. It includes a stylistic analysis of the rondolike musical structure of the monologue and its four verbal music episodes (verbal equivalents of a toccata, fugue, and two cadenzas), as well as a reader-response-oriented interpretation of the text. Preliminary sections of the dissertation deal with the use of musical language in fiction as a modernistic device; the concept of the lyrical novel; and Hildesheimer's essays on the absurd (6-27). *Tynset* is not literature of the absurd, Haas claims, but it has some features in common with that genre, including the narrator's basically absurd outlook. This outlook resembles that of the lyrical "I," for whom objectivity is also essential. The narrator's passivity and the absence of pathos in his revelations are features common to both genres (8, 105-11). (See Puknus 1978, 125, for an opposing opinion.)

The categories of literary language that appear in the *Tynset* rondo are: (1) verbal music, (2) impersonal storytelling (the episodes), and (3) a reflective style that includes objective and subjective lyricism (the refrains). The following stylistic elements occur throughout the text:

> (1) highly articulate, associational "free prose," whose rhythmic structure is the phrase and clause rather than the sentence; (2) verbal rather than nominal structure (145).

In Part 3, Chapter 2, Haas analyzes the episodes and reflective passages that reveal the narrator's isolation-alienation, which is the main theme of the literary rondo. Secondary themes include

> brutality of man, fear of interpersonal relationships, the impersonality of city life, rigidity of Christian religion, and man's inability to help his fellow man (32).

The brutality theme, composed of brief and often indirect allusions, contains the historical-political element that, according to Domin, is both everpresent and simultaneously not present at all in *Tynset* (1965, 124). Haas also addresses the issue of the narrator's "insistence on innocence" and asserts that it is a part of his absurd worldview: guilt and innocence are no longer clearly definable after the Third Reich, "which expanded the consciousness of the world" (110). Giles Hoyt says much the same thing: "In the absurd post-Auschwitz world justice does not seem possible, since ethical correlatives are shown to be false" (1978, 133).

The narrator has no guilt in a world without justice, and he therefore has no motivation to act. Instead, he makes new myths and destroys old ones in his attempt to define reality. Goll-Bickmann's dimensional examination of the passive narrator's innocence, which contains no reference to Hoyt, actually develops the Hoyt discussion of myth-making. Hoyt also anticipates Rath's semiotic study when he notes that language alone in an absurd world remains intact, "since it does not undergo the inversion or alienation that the rest of the world does" (138).

Hoyt's article is valuable because it shifts our attention from the narrator to the aesthetic realm of the text itself. Although Haas concludes that the "lyrical modality" of *Tynset*, disciplined as it is by musical structure, offers a challenge to "enter the abstract transcendent universe of modernism" (1975, 216), she focuses on the narrator.

Hoyt, Goll-Bickmann, and Rath concentrate on the narrator's discourse, subjecting it to a close – sometimes fanciful – reading. Rath, for example, perceives that the narrator's alienation is manifested particularly in the place-name Tynset, which is more important than the related name Hamlet. Tynset is a metaphor of recognition and of mystery (1985, 102-10), a motive of both rest from tension and beginnings (121-34), and a metaphor for life as well as the beginning and the end (143-50). Initially, Rath devotes some space to diagramming the wavelike flow of the text and the breathy quality of material within a wave (90-98), but the various binary oppositions he identifies establish a textual openness that is his contribution to Hildesheimer research.

Rath also gives a mythological background to the narrator's misery as he introduces comparisons with Greek and Indian mythology, the biblical story of Adam and Eve and the Tree of Knowledge, and numerous German and French texts. Unfortunately, Rath does not support his identification of the book as a novel in stream-of-consciousness form, and his conclusion is weak. He decides that the interior dialogue is half-hearted, for the writer simply reproduces what he criticizes (161). A reader interested in semiotics might enjoy the lengthy discussion of the y in *Tynset* (134-43). Otherwise, apart from the instructive binarisms, there are too many abstract formulations and rhetorical questions and too few substantive statements in Rath's book.

For Christiaan Hart-Nibbrig the language of *Tynset* resembles the score of a musical composition. Like the narrator of the book, who equates syllables with tones, Hart-Nibbrig hears music in individual words and in the descriptions of the concert of roosters and the summer bed fugue, where chronological time disappears and a past event becomes immediate (1976, 1202).

The essay is a tribute to Hildesheimer on his sixtieth birthday and is generally impressionistic. Hart-Nibbrig labels the text unique for its musicality and pessimism and asserts that no other contemporary writer, including Frisch, Handke, Grass, Koeppen, Johnson, Walser, or Bernhard, has succeeded like Hildesheimer in transposing the content of subjective experiences into an objective structure (1207).

In an essay honoring Hildesheimer on his seventieth birthday Reichert includes *Tynset* in a sweeping claim that the writer's prose landscapes are stage sets where scenes are played out in isolation and images become fixed as Baroque emblems of such monstrous concepts as death and failure. Reichert also refers to another Baroque device, the allegory, which he feels is the real key to understanding what Hildesheimer has to say (1987, 77-78). His comments suggest further avenues for investigation.

Neither Goll-Bickmann, Rath, nor Hart-Nibbrig chooses to investigate the absurd elements in *Tynset*, but there is ample support for the Haas and Hoyt indications of the narrator's absurd outlook in Nef, Dücker, Andersson's 1979 study of alienation, and the section of Blamberger's book, *Versuch über den deutschen Gegenwartsroman* (Experimental Discussion of the German Contemporary Novel, 1985), devoted to Hildesheimer's work. Blamberger's 1986 article, "Der Rest ist Schweigen" (All That is Left is Silence), is a distillation of the earlier text, together with new material pertaining to the plays.

Although Nef does not specifically identify *Tynset* as a work of the absurd, he does consider the summer bed fugue as representative of Hildesheimer's concept of the absurd. In this episode seven people die of the plague in the massive bed in which each exhibits an outstanding asocial characteristic (greed, lust, etc.). Unknown to and thus isolated from each other, these seven are united for a night in the bed in which they will die. They illustrate the contradiction between the laws of common sense and the nonfulfillment of those laws, between being free from laws while at the same time being bound to them. The fugue is a paradigm of Hildesheimer's absurd world view (1975, 38-39). Nef's point is well taken.

In his basically sociological approach to Hildesheimer's texts, Dücker claims that the *Tynset* narrator isolates himself from the world because of his certainty that the terrors of the Nazi era are repeatable. This certainty establishes that the world in which he lives is absurd. Dücker, however, compares the narrator to German literary figures (Böll's Hans Schnier, Frisch's Stiller) who are similarly intellectual and reflective, rather than to other absurd narrators; in fact, he says nothing more about the absurd in his short discussion of *Tynset* (1976, 83-88). Instead, he develops Kähler's comments on the imperialistic capitalism of contemporary West Germany and the continued existence of inhumane fascism in the West. Dücker concentrates on the descriptive eloquence and circularity of the melancholy narrator's memories of the Nazi past and his opinion that value systems from that time reemerge in society (1976, 85; Kähler 1965, 792, 795). Goll-Bickmann later amplifies two of Dücker's revelations: that the narrator's melancholy is caused by renunciation of specific action in light of his view of society, and that the narrator tries to compensate for his renunciation with stream-of-consciousness memories and reflections (Dücker 1976, 87; Goll-Bickmann 1989, 248-61, 290-93).

Andersson, too, refers to Kähler's essay, which he amends and contradicts. To the East German critic's claim that *Tynset* is comparable in some ways to Beckett's *Waiting for Godot*, Andersson adds that both Godot and Tynset are unknowns. Both function psychologically as concrete possibilities for connectedness in an otherwise evanescent world and are significant because they are possible goals. They give meaning to life in a confusing world (1979, 142; Kähler 1965, 793).

Andersson's disagreement with the Kähler comment that Hildesheimer sees no development in history is reflected in his interpretation of the Hamlet figure. The narrator does not accept the challenge to action proffered by the silent ghost of Hamlet's father because the alternative to the present would not be any better, and it would still encompass death. The narrator accepts no ordering of life that recognizes death (157-60; Kähler 1965, 793). This interpretation is related to what Andersson sees as a godlike characteristic: the narrator believes in nothing but his own disbelief, and in his solipsism he worships his own religion of disavowal (107). (See Goll-Bickmann 1989, 262-90, for a complicated discussion of the multiple godlike roles the narrator assumes; see Puknus 1978, 68, for another reference to solipsism.)

In Andersson's reading of *Tynset* the image of the world is not, as Kähler argues, static. Social change may be possible, but it is a relative development – from inhumane to less inhumane. The narrator is lost in a world that remains silent but that has created a God and with that God an immoral church and religious charlatans who preach a substitute answer that they use as a reward for order. The narrator is opposed to this God and his protectors and preachers, and he is opposed to the susceptibility of people to a message that seduces. In spite of everything, however, the possibility remains that to be less inhumane is the only alternative, even though the narrator himself cannot accept it (1979, 165).

Andersson incorporates Hildesheimer's definition of the absurd into his interpretation, adding as his contribution the possibility of inhumane social change. He explains why – in *Tynset* and other Hildesheimer texts – the problematic of alienation must be examined together with the problematic of the absurd: alienation for a Hildesheimer narrator means that human activity as a social reality is meaningless in a world where the laws of all social systems and religions have no meaning. Hildesheimer begins with the problematic of the inhumanity of society, but as he considers morality he comes to unanswerable metaphysical questions. For this reason he is sometimes regarded as a social critic and sometimes as an absurdist. The alienation of the individual in society becomes generalized into the feeling that humanity is an alien in the world. Alienation opens up a problematic that reaches from its social aspect into the metaphysical (13-14).

Blamberger regards all of Hildesheimer's prose as absurd in orientation. The narrator is not writing to prove the reality of the absurd to himself but to instruct the reader, for many people are not aware of its pervasiveness (1985, 86). Blamberger emphasizes the close connection between author and narrator as an indicator of the absurd, but that does not mean that *Tynset* and *Masante* are autobiographical books. The author of absurd prose is identifiable as the narrator in only one respect: both experience reality as absurd (84). Blamberger erroneously finds two additional points of resemblance between Hildesheimer and his narrator: both are writers, and both are Jews living in exile (83, 91). There is no indication in either book that the narrator is a professional writer. Although he alludes to his Jewish heritage in *Tynset* and lives in a self-imposed exile, there are no such references in *Masante*. Hildesheimer does not use the word *exile* in his discourse, and he has said that he never considered himself to be in exile (Durzak 1976, 271-72).

Blamberger's interpretation of the labyrinth motive in *Tynset* suggests a new avenue of exploration. God's rejection of Cain's gift indicates to the narrator how arbitrarily God acts and how useless it is to attempt to orient oneself in the world. The narrator regards the world, therefore, as a labyrinthine type of cage (1985, 89). Blamberger contrasts Hildesheimer's labyrinth images with like representations in mythology and in Mannerism in sixteenth-century art. Mythological labyrinths always signify a continuation from death into a new life. In Mannerism the labyrinth is a symbol of the unreasonableness of God's world. The artist of that period juxtaposed to this unreasonableness various artificial worlds whose arbitrariness he himself, as an "alter deus," could determine. In *Tynset* thoughts of death occur in labyrinth scenes, but there is never any reference to an afterlife. Hildesheimer's labyrinth images signify confusion ("Irrgang") and loss of freedom but never continuation beyond death. The narrator does not attempt to play God by creating worlds of his own; what he tries to create is emptiness (88-89), an insight that Petuchowski expressed as early as 1975 and with which Andersson and Goll-Bickmann would, of course, disagree. (For a contrasting view of Blamberger's references to Mannerism, see Heidsieck 1969, 28-36.)

Several scholars who, like Kähler and Dücker, are interested in the social history in *Tynset*, incorporate biographical or autobiographical considerations in readings that ignore or reject the issue of the absurd. Henry A. Lea published two such essays (in 1979 and 1989), in the second of which he reveals that he, like Hildesheimer, was a translator at the Nuremberg War Crimes Trials. This new information is extremely useful and narratologically intriguing.

Lea's thesis is that *Tynset* and *Masante* are examples of exile literature that reveal the narrator's fear and anxiety about his former homeland. In the most illustrative episode of the earlier text the narrator attempts to drive through the city he decides to call "Wilhelmstadt" (Hildesheimer 1965c, 114; 1991a, 2, 67). Most significant in his narrative are the fear and alienation he reveals and "his description of the city as a labyrinth and a citadel of rampant nationalism" (Lea 1979, 22). Lea explains the origin of all place names, and, with only one exception, the street names are indeed nationalistic and "directly related to the Nazi years" (1979, 24). The exception is "die Judengasse" (Jew's Alley), to which the narrator appends "wo ich hingehöre" (where I belong) (Hildesheimer 1965c, 118; 1991a, 2, 69-70), one of few personal remarks in the text (see Haas 1975, 93-95).

Lea also points out that the geographical locations in both books are real places that are "border" areas, "geographic as well as existential." All are defined "by their physical and psychological distance from Germany" (1979, 21). Hildesheimer thus establishes the exile situation of his narrator. Lea is in error, however, when he says that Hildesheimer himself had to leave Germany "under pressure of persecution" and "has twice gone into exile, the second time voluntarily" (26). Hildesheimer did not live in exile. He told Durzak that his family left Germany before the Nazis began to exert their power and simply because his parents wanted to move to England. He was never in exile, he said, and he has never experienced feelings of exile (Durzak 1976, 271-72).

Lea assumes that because the Hildesheimer family is Jewish, anti-Semitism and fear of persecution prompted the family's departure from Germany in 1933. In the 1989 article he writes that anti-Semitism seems to be the reason Hildesheimer left Germany for a village in Switzerland in 1957. To support this supposition, he quotes from an interview with Marcel Reich-Ranicki (published in 1973) in which Hildesheimer categorically states that two-thirds of all Germans are and have always been anti-Semitic (Lea 1989, 51). But Hans Werner Richter, founder of Gruppe 47 and personally acquainted with Hildesheimer in 1957, would object to Lea's assumption. He reports that Hildesheimer, who had recently married, felt that his wife's health would benefit from their move to the rural and less noisy environment of a Swiss village (Richter 1986, 143).

The writer himself rebuts Lea's assumption that the Hildesheimer family left Germany unwillingly in his entry for the book *Mein Judentum* (My Jewishness, 1978), in which twenty-one writers describe what it is like to be a Jew. His family never experienced anti-Semitism, Hildesheimer says. His father, a Zionist who had wanted to live in Palestine since at least 1929, decided to move the family there from England in 1933. They were not forced to leave Germany because they feared persecution (1991a, 7, 160-62). The writer himself did not experience anti-Semitism, either as a boy or later, and it was only at Nuremberg that he learned the extent of racial hatred in Germany (164). Anyone who attempts to interpret Hildesheimer's reflective works from a biographical standpoint should read this unusually revealing document.

In the 1989 essay Lea contradicts himself. He says that *Tynset* is autobiographical but later describes the book as a mixture of reality and fiction in which reality predominates (51, 53). In the 1979 article he implies an autobiographical content for *Tynset* by continually juxtaposing biographical data and fictional events. What seems to be indecisiveness is based on personal involvement so unusual that it may be impossible for this scholar to evade the intentional fallacy that comes into play in both his essays. At Nuremberg he and Hildesheimer translated testimony of the prisoners into English. He believes that such a translator would become aware of the actual content of the testimony only years later, for at the time of translation one would be too involved with grammatical issues to focus on the import of the spoken words. One might even repress the content of what he heard in order to remain objective as he translated. If it is possible for a Jewish writer who was born in Germany to deal with material from the trials in a literary way, it is only possible, Lea writes, after years have passed and only in the form of a highly personal commentary (1989, 51). Lea's perspective, which is undoubtedly affected (unconsciously, to be sure) by his own response to the experience he shared with Hildesheimer, is unprecedented in Hildesheimer criticism and of interest to narratologists as well as to critics who favor a psychoanalytical approach.

Blamberger would agree that one could easily identify *Tynset's* narrator as the author, but he prefers to regard the many similarities between the two as necessitated by their common realization that reality is an absurd construct (1985, 84). Lea rejects out of hand any claim that Hildesheimer is an absurdist (including the writer's own statements to that effect) because his prose is essayistic rather than descriptive and lacks the free play of the imagination that one finds in such acknowledged absurdists as Ionesco and Beckett (1989, 45-46). (See Chapter 4 below for development of this last issue.)

Hanenberg, who generally concentrates on the historical value of *Tynset*, proposes another autobiographically tinged reading by linking *Tynset* to the short, seemingly autobiographical text, "Die Margarinefabrik" (The Margarine Factory), which was published in 1965 in a collection of stories titled *Atlas* (see Hildesheimer 1991a, 1, 303-12; Hanenberg 1989, 134-36). Petuchowski, in a brief reference to the text, describes it as "so far, the most serene from Hildesheimer's pen" (1975, 83). The narrator describes an abandoned margarine factory in a Norwegian town whose name he does not remember. He senses an absence of history in the peaceful silence of this town and recalls that his father managed and even once built a margarine factory.

The abandoned building offers the fulfillment that the narrator in *Tynset* seeks but does not find, Hanenberg suggests, because painful memories of his murdered father (represented by the ghost of Hamlet's father) keep him from fleeing to Tynset (another town in Norway). Thinking about his father in the empty factory, however, does not disturb the narrator; in fact, the margarine factory serves as a memorial to his father. The narrator can flee from the horror of the past and even forget it only where he can feel his dead father's presence. Hanenberg ends his interpretation with three rhetorical questions that compel the reader to contradict his autobiographical intimation. Is the father figure in both texts identical? Is the narrator able to forget the past in the nameless town because his father is memorialized there in the abandoned factory? If the two texts were read together, would they be parts of an autobiographical answer (135-36)? If the narrator of the short text finds no trace of German barbarism in the nameless Norwegian town, not even when he thinks about his father, it seems obvious that that father cannot be compared with the *Tynset* narrator's father, who was killed by Nazis.

Hanenberg's final question can also be answered by referring to the *Gesammelte Werke*, where the short story is included in Volume 1, which contains narrative texts, rather than Volume 7, devoted to personal, essayistic pieces. There is no volume of autobiographical texts in the collection. *Tynset* and *Masante* occupy Volume 2, "Monologische Prosa" (monological prose), which attests somewhat ambiguously to their fictionality.

Hanenberg asserts categorically that *Tynset* is not a novel because its content – memories of Germany's past – precludes all fictionalizing (133), a point that Lea also makes (1989, 53). The efforts of both these critics to label the book as autobiographical must remain unsuccessful, however, based on the contradictory evidence examined here.

Jehle advises the reader of *Tynset* not to look for autobiographical references (1990, 93, 95). With this remark he tacitly contradicts the Lea essay of 1989, which was published in a collection he edited and must have been known to him.

The volume and range of interpretations surrounding *Tynset* establish the complexity of its issues and the advisability of applying varied theoretical positions to a text that is obviously not easily categorized. *Tynset* is not a traditional novel. It is not an autobiography, either, despite its revelations. It is not exile literature, if the author himself is to be believed. It is not absurd literature, although its narrator has an absurd worldview. Critics generally agree that the text is reflective and has a lyrical tone, and for these reasons it resembles works by Hermann Hesse, André Gide, and Virginia Woolf. Ralph Freedman's discussion of these writers in *The Lyrical Novel* (1971) might be helpful in understanding *Tynset*.

The *Tynset* narrator is comparable to the narrator of *Vergebliche Aufzeichnungen*, especially when one considers the Hamlet references in the later text, as nearly every critic does. *Vergebliche Aufzeichnungen* is also neither a novel nor an autobiography. In both reflective texts (which seems to be the most neutral way to treat them) an articulate, artistic, well-educated man describes, more or less explicitly, his feelings of isolation and alienation. The *Tynset* narrator clarifies the alienation we perceive in the earlier work as he recounts events of religious, historical, political, and humanistic significance not only to Germans and those of Jewish heritage but to any human being. In this respect *Tynset* is a work of world literature, as Haas (1975) and Goll-Bickmann (1989) demonstrate.

What distinguishes *Tynset* from all prior or later Hildesheimer texts is the musical structure of the book, especially the verbal-music episodes. Although Koebner (1971) and Rath (1985) describe the prose as a stream of consciousness, Haas (1975) details the musical principles that specifically determine the syntax. Petuchowski (1975), Haas, and Goll-Bickmann (1989) discuss the causality behind the flow of thoughts from reflective passages into self-contained storytelling episodes and back again into reflective passages. What Rath and, before him, Kähler (1965) and Dücker (1976) describe as the wavelike movement of this material is carefully controlled with regard to the presentation of images.

The historical relevance of *Tynset* is apparent thanks to the work of Lea (1979, 1989) and Hanenberg (1989). The text is comparable to Rolf Hochhuth's 1963 drama, *Der Stellvertreter* (translated as *The Deputy*), as well as to Ilse Aichinger's novel, *Die größere Hoffnung* (The Greater Hope, 1948), and Elie Wiesel's *La Nuit* (translated as *Night*, 1958), all three of which disclose nightmare experiences in Nazi Germany. If *Tynset* has not yet found its place in literary discussions of the Holocaust, it is perhaps because of its musical structure and the absurd orientation of its narrator. Future research might focus on the comparisons noted above.

Tynset is not merely a book about Germany, however, and it is not entirely suited to the context in which Durzak (1976), Blamberger (1985), and Rath (1985) situate their discussions. Comparisons with German novels of the 1960s leave areas unexplored that would be illuminated if Hildesheimer's relationship to Camus, Joyce, Beckett, Ionesco, Barnes, Woolf, and Borges were developed. The use of musical principles and devices by Hildesheimer and Beckett, for instance, deserves study. Beckett gives musical stage directions in *Play* ("da capo" to indicate repetition of the text, "choral" to describe the opening passage), and Croak in *Words and Music* pleads for friendship between the necessary elements of song. Eugene Kaelin, who discusses these texts, notes that the rhythmic sound in the television play *Breath* is equivalent to the "pulse of life" (1981, 265). Beckett's intimations of the relationship between music and life itself and Hildesheimer's use of a musical vocabulary in his existential monologue are topics that deserve comparative analysis.

The final suggestion of the present work is to free *Tynset* from autobiographical claims and read it as a postmodern text. This suggestion applies to nearly all of Hildesheimer's oeuvre.

C. *Masante*

In a 1971 interview with Walter Jens, Hildesheimer was reminded that he had said he had nothing more to say after *Tynset* and would return to painting. The author replied that there was much he wanted to put into *Tynset* that could not be accommodated; he decided, therefore, to write a new book (Jens 1971a, 95).

Hildesheimer titled the successor book *Meona*, and it was to have been published in 1969 (Jehle 1990, 109). Instead, the radio play *Maxine*, based on the female figure of the work-in-progress, appeared that year, and Hildesheimer continued to work on the book. Additional material was published in 1971 as *Zeiten in Cornwall* (Times in Cornwall). Finally, the book title was changed to *Masante*, and it was published in 1973.

Hildesheimer explained in the Durzak interview of 1976 that as he worked on *Meona* he felt so overwhelmed by the quantity of material he had, even after writing *Maxine*, that he sought the advice of Dierk Rodewald, his first archivist. Rodewald encouraged him to extract the autobiographical material and create a separate work, which became *Zeiten in Cornwall*. The author then rewrote the manuscript and requested critical comments from a publisher's reader as well as from Peter Horst Neumann, the literary critic, and Jens, himself a novelist as well as professor of literature at the University of Tübingen (Durzak 1976, 282). The dust jacket of the book identifies it as a novel, but Hildesheimer did not give it this designation, although he admitted that the book is more novelistic than *Tynset* (287).

The critical success of *Tynset* and the literary prizes it received guaranteed that *Masante* would be eagerly awaited and promptly reviewed; but, perhaps because *Tynset* was not a commercial success, there are fewer reviews listed in Jehle's *Bibliographie* (1984, 183-90). Of the early reviewers Geno Hartlaub, Peter Wapnewski, and Neumann offer insights developed later by others. Hartlaub describes *Masante* as more difficult to read than *Tynset*, because it is more radical and abstract. The social criticism presented is far more effective than any found in the politically oriented German literature of the time (1989, 262-63). Wapnewski (whose review is distinguished by pregnant observations in sentence fragments) mentions the magic of Hildesheimer's talent for names. He describes *Masante* as a "poetische Enzyklopädie" (1973, 324-26), a term taken up by nearly every later critic. Neumann compares the quality of narration in *Masante* (and *Tynset*) to that in works by Kafka and Cervantes. Like the melancholy Don Quixote, the *Masante* narrator observes no clear distinction between reality and fiction. As a consequence, *Masante* becomes Kafkaesque in at least two particulars: the unyielding candor of its self-observations and the presence of two pursuers ("Häscher"). Neumann also refers to Beckett and Günter Eich. Hildesheimer's confessional prose tries to hide its revelations behind cynicism, black humor, and a coolly pointed speech that resembles discourse by both those writers (496). Neumann speculates that *Masante*, a book whose theme is failure, succeeds – paradoxically – because Hildesheimer has given his narrator a congenial conversational partner equally steeped in failure but also equally intelligent. Maxine might, in fact, be called a projection of the narrator (497).

Maxine and the "Häscher" are the most frequently discussed elements of *Masante*. The studies evaluated below generally take either a psychological (Maxine) or historical ("Häscher") approach, but in two notable exceptions *Masante* is treated as literature of the absurd.

In her 1975 dissertation Petuchowski has much to say about Maxine, but it is not always clear or cogent. She claims, for example, that the narrator remains isolated and detached from everyone at the desert inn, including Maxine, because they are all his creations. "The narrator fills an empty stage with characters; a stage designer sees the inn from the draftsman's viewpoint" (142). (The latter observation undoubtedly relates to Hildesheimer's study of cabinetmaking and furniture and stage design in London and Jerusalem from 1934 to 1939.) Petuchowski points out several theatrical terms in the text to support her contention that the narrator "as playwright" creates Maxine as his alter ego (131). And yet, even though she says that the relationship between these two is "not, in the positive meaning, a human relationship" (142), Petuchowski remarks later that it is "paradoxically" distant (144) but does not explain why. She does, however, remind us of the many traits and experiences shared by the narrator and Maxine, and her delineation of the images of emptiness in the book is useful for anyone taking a psychological approach to the text.

Petuchowski's references to stage directions and other theatrical terms are echoed by Reichert, who makes several theatrical comparisons in his commemorative essay of 1987. He likens the narrator's disappearance into the desert, for instance, to a stage exit (80). His observations and Petuchowski's suggest that Hildesheimer's training as a stage designer plays a more efficacious role in his prose than in his dramas. (See Chapter 4 below for discussion of Hildesheimer as a dramatist whose plays are too static for the stage.)

In a collection of essays titled *Zwischen Entfremdung und Utopie: Die Neuentdeckung des Poetischen* (Between Alienation and Utopia: The New Poetic Discovery, 1975), Paul Konrad Kurz limits his evaluation of *Masante* to the narrator's interest in saints and saintliness. Maxine is not a sinner at all, the narrator decides, but one of the real saints (Hildesheimer 1973, 350; 1991a, 2, 351). Kurz advances the unique notion that *Masante* should be read as if it were a modern Book of Ecclesiastes, even though Hildesheimer, as a modern preacher, is an intellectual. The impetus for his idea is the realization voiced by the narrator of the biblical text and

Masante that to strive is useless, for everything in life is vain (1975, 75). Kurz does not make the following observation, but the contradictory statements about wisdom in Ecclesiastes 9:15-18 might be applied to Alain, Maxine, and even the narrator himself if one were to develop the Kurz idea and answer his rhetorical question, why does the narrator – who professes not to believe in God – have such an interest in saints?

According to Stanley (1994), the saints, who respond to an inner voice, represent the opposite of the "Häscher," who follow orders. The narrator hangs the religious calendar on his wall to remind him of the distinction. His interest focuses on the strength of the saints' inner voice. If there is any hope for the future, it is in cultivating such an inner voice in each of us, but the narrator is not thereby advocating a religious response. By becoming so involved in brief literary evocations of music and paintings in his storytelling that he forgets his fear of the "Häscher," he shows us that it is art, both visual and musical, and not religion that gives him strength.

Nef's reading of *Masante* is also provocative. He claims that the "Häscher" are not specific persons and that they appear within no specific historical period, for they are projections of the narrator's persecution complex, images incorporating his reason for anxiety and fright in a reality that is incomprehensible to him. The confident brutality of the "Häscher," who are convinced that they understand the world, is diametrically opposed to the narrator's fear (1975, 41-42). Although Nef does not mention Martin Heidegger's concept of inauthenticity, his remark that the "Häscher" in their blind certainty are typical of the active participants of this world suggests a Heideggerian orientation.

Dücker notices that the narrator and Maxine do not communicate but merely exchange monologues. The woman serves as a contrast to the narrator, for she seeks nothing in life; she simply drinks, sleeps, and waits for the end. The narrator, on the other hand, makes an attempt to find an authentic existence. The attempt is doomed from the beginning, and Dücker compares the text in this respect to one of Hildesheimer's earliest stories, "Das Ende einer Welt." He also compares *Masante* and *Tynset* to *Vergebliche Aufzeichnungen,* for in all three reflective texts the narrator understands that it is vain to look for completion or answers in the "Stoff" (substance) of existence. The last of the three texts is not critical of society but of self. The narrator berates himself for his own incompetence and inability to make use of what he has learned about life (1976, 100-2). According to Dücker, the framework of *Masante* reveals not only the narrator's personal history but the history of Western culture. Associative leaps in thought reflect the encyclopedic nature of the narrator's intellectual background, he says – a perceptive comment that anticipates responses to *Marbot* several years later.

Durzak (like Hartlaub in his early review) uses the comparative of "radikal" when he compares *Masante* to *Tynset*. The "Häscher" motive is so much more radically anchored in German history that the narrator no longer needs to transpose it into the Hamlet material, as he does in *Tynset*. Instead of developing what he sees as the narrator's dystopic view of contemporary Germany embodied in the "Häscher" motive, however, Durzak decides that Hildesheimer merely transposes the two "Häscher" into equivalents of the men in Kafka's *Der Prozeß* (*The Trial*) who lead Josef K. to his death. Durzak's evaluation then becomes a biographical, quasi-psychological inquiry as he wonders whether the author is merely bemoaning his own situation in what is nothing more than a literary exercise and allowing his experiences to overpower the social and political background of the novel so that its significance shrinks from potentially universal to personal (1976, 308-11).

Arens makes somewhat the same point when she faults Hildesheimer for ignoring the social implications in his Mozart biography, but in her opinion the writer's shortcomings reflect a general postwar German attitude (1986, 167). How Hildesheimer functions as a social critic in his fictional texts could be a worthwhile subject for future research. His narrative "I" is not merely indulging in a literary exercise, as Durzak speculates.

The key to interpreting *Masante* appears in the name of the book, Puknus claims. Once we understand why *Meona*, the original title, was changed, we discard any notion that the book is merely a variation or imitation of *Tynset*. Cal Masante, the house in Italy that the narrator leaves to travel to Meona, should not be confused with the house in *Tynset*. There were tormenting memories in the latter house that paralyzed the narrator, making it impossible for him to leave it or even his bed. Cal Masante has no such memories, and the narrator freely leaves it to travel to the desert. In Meona he regards his house in Italy as a refuge from the society to which he wants to, and can, return whenever he wishes, but it is significant that he carried out a decision to leave the house (1978, 102).

Consonant with his theory, Puknus declares that this narrator is no longer solipsistic. His worries ("Nöte") are as important as ever to him, but he is also able to comment and reflect on what Alain and Maxine relate. Puknus uses the term "weltoffener" (more open to the world) to describe the narrator's sociability. He has people around him in this text; and he takes more notice than in *Tynset* of historical, geographical, and timely events, which he describes or around which he creates stories that could be real. For this reason, Puknus agrees with Wapnewski's term, "poetische Enzyklopädie," as a metaphor for the work. The "Häscher" are remarkable for Puknus mainly because their names are so suitable. They are simply characters in stories that could be real (104-6).

In an essay that also appeared in 1978 Christoph Eykman unintentionally attempts to expand the meaning of *weltoffener* by describing the double perspective (with its element of "doppelter Optik") that occurs when the narrator incorporates imagery from works of art and literature to enhance his descriptions of, for example, the green of a Christmas tree and the physical appearance of the two "Häscher." The narrator's situation gains credibility as "real" when the educated reader adds knowledge of the items mentioned – Manet's bucolic "Le Dejeuner en l'Herbe" and Kafka's novel *Der Prozeß* – to what the narrator has described. The narrator's invented world opens up when he brings into it the "außerfiktionale Realelement"(extrafictional real element) of a painting or book (328-30).

Eykman's references to *Masante* are brief, for he also examines fiction by Alfred Döblin and Alexander Kluge. His thesis may be valid for the other texts, but his argument is not convincing for *Masante* because he posits a generalized reader response. A Hildesheimer reader is not apt to ignore the inaccuracies in the narrator's description of the real items, which is what Eykman implies by not dealing with them himself. For such a reader the text surely does not become more real. Watt's study of the implied Hildesheimer reader appeared five years after Eykman's article (see Chapter 1 above); but even if Eykman could not have been aware that the average reader was not the implied reader of a Hildesheimer text he could have known that his hypothetical educated reader was not the actual purchaser of Hildesheimer's books, for no book prior to *Mozart* (1977) sold well.

Heinz Wetzel's 1979 essay, which is based on an entirely different approach to the "real" and foreshadows the work of Blamberger (1985) and Hanenberg (1989), is far more valuable. Wetzel writes that the narrator does not want events or persons from the Nazi era to be real to the reader. He wants them to be typical: neither actually recalled nor purely fictional. The narrator accomplishes this effect by suggesting possible changes to an event or other names for the "Häscher." With these suggestions he invites the reader to participate in his effort to concretize a typical event or type of person (148-49). The events and characters are real, but they become paradigms of events and people as they are written down, and in that way they can, presumably, be set aside. The narrator's goal is to free himself from his oppressive past experiences by giving each pursuer a name that suits him or by giving a remembered name a form that fits it. The narrator fails to write his experiences out of his life, in spite of his linguistically interesting efforts, because the "Häscher" have too strong a hold on Western society. They are as much a part of the order of things as the saints named on the narrator's religious calendar (159-61).

Wetzel compares the names of the "Häscher" to the names on the desert signposts in the following way: as long as the narrator orients himself by means of the "Häscher" names, he is not free; he tries, by writing, to rid himself of the unpleasant associations tied to the "Häscher." As long as he orients himself in the desert by means of the signposts, he is not really lost. Without the "Häscher" and the signpost names, the narrator is fully free and also fully lost. To be fully lost, as in sleep, is his alternative wish, if he cannot free himself from the "Häscher." At the end of *Masante* we do not know whether he will die in the desert sandstorm or find an orienting signpost and return to the inn, where he can resume his frustrated (and frustrating) attempts to free himself from his past. It is possible that Hildesheimer's narrator could find his way out of the desert and appear in another narrative. Perhaps at a later time readers would recognize the significance of his efforts (162). Wetzel's reading might be influenced by the fact that a guest at the inn does return from the desert in the radio play *Maxine* (see Hildesheimer 1991a, 5, 396).

Andersson, who also has a positive qua hopeful interpretation of *Masante*, disregards the narrator's decision to go into the desert altogether and discusses the visit to Meona as a learning experience from which the narrator will profit. Certain that his search for a valid answer is useless, the narrator will live with the knowledge that he has failed and will not be dominated by the wish to find an answer (1979, 126-27).

Wetzel does not develop his claim that the "Häscher" represent Western society, but he does show that their names may be tied to events of the Nazi past. The associations that he finds in the phonetic structure of "Stollfuß" are remarkable and indicative of the significance of this book for Wetzel himself, who concludes that the name of this particular pursuer personifies historical progress from the nationalistic conservatism of a Dollfuß (the Austrian minister president who was murdered by Austrian Nazis in 1934) to the terror of a Goebbels (1979, 156).

According to Wetzel, the narrator tries unsuccessfully to regard his pursuers as harmless by calling them "Häscher" rather than "Verfolger" (pursuer, 152). According to Lea, however, "Häscher" is synonymous in modern usage with "Verfolger" (1979, 23), and it is thus an equally sinister name.

Lea's opinion of the narrator's disappearance in the desert is radically different. The narrator dies in a desert that symbolizes both a return to his Jewish origin (since Israel is in the desert – although this fact does not appear in the text) and an escape from his German heritage, which he satirizes in quotations and proverbs throughout the book. The fear and restlessness that pervade the monologue are "surface symptoms" of the narrator's exiled condition (1979, 26).

Lea's interpretation of *Tynset* and *Masante* is uniquely biographical. He views the texts as exile literature and as witnesses to Hildesheimer's rejection of West Germany, "mainly because he finds it pervasively and unregenerately anti-Semitic" (26). Lea is, unfortunately, too intent on his biographical argument to explain for non-German readers the significance of several proverbs in the text. The reader must simply take his word for it that they have a satirical aim. In spite of this omission and even if one does not agree that Hildesheimer lives in exile, the two Lea articles remain valuable for their most unusual perspective and for the information they contain that links both texts to German social history.

Equally valuable is Blamberger's impressively cogent thesis that all of Hildesheimer's fictional work is based on an absurd worldview that is most evident in *Masante*. The narrator gives up his efforts to unmask the absurd and concludes that it is impossible to arrive at an absolute meaning, an "Urtext" (original text) for living. All he finds are lies or variations on truth. When these are taken apart there is still no basic text – no answers – at least not for him. Others are able to get around in the world, but not this continually frustrated narrator. His death in the desert is meant to signal the death of the modern novel and the end – for Hildesheimer himself – of absurd prose in novel form (1985, 98).

Blamberger is not the only critic who regards *Masante* as a work of absurd prose, but his interpretation is the most convincing. Rath, whose study of the contemporary German novel also appeared in 1985, agrees that Hildesheimer writes in the tradition of the absurd, employing a prose style that blends monomaniacal melancholy with satire (79). Since Rath is mainly interested in the language of *Tynset*, he seldom refers to the later text. Blamberger, who constantly shifts from *Tynset* to *Masante*, supports his claim that both texts are absurd with a valuable discussion of the narrator's identification with Hamlet, who has appeared in all of Hildesheimer's larger works of fiction. The *Tynset* and *Masante* narrator yearns, like Hamlet, to forget the horrors of life in sleep, and he exhibits a melancholy similar to Hamlet's; but it has a different origin. Hamlet's melancholy is based on the guilt he feels because he cannot act against his father's murderer and become a murderer

himself. Instead he becomes a fool in the hope that he can unmask
the murderer with words. The narrator in *Tynset* turns away from
the silent challenge to act in the son's stead incorporated in the
ghost of Hamlet's father, for he believes that only renunciation of
any kind of action can give one a sense of guiltlessness. He is not,
however, convinced until *Masante* that his passive response to the
horrors of life is his only possible response. By going out into the
desert to his death he tacitly dismisses Hamlet's reliance on words
to unmask horror, but he retains throughout the text Hamlet's
melancholy cognition of life's horror, which is for him the representation of the absurd (94-95). (See Hoyt 1978, 133-40, for another
discussion of guiltlessness.)

Blamberger views Maxine as a second absurd "I" and a sometime replacement for the narrator as the figure with which the
author identifies (85). He does not notice that if she is indeed a
replacement figure she displays a characteristic markedly different
from those of the narrator: he is preoccupied with contemplation
of death, while her stories are about life. It is a weakness of Hildesheimer's writing, according to Blamberger, that the narrator cannot
think of death as amorphous but must give it a shape and imagines
that it will appear in various locations (90). If *Tynset* and *Masante*
are the working out of a single writing plan, Maxine's life-affirm-
ing stories deserve more attention as an indicator of a tendency
toward hope that emerges from time to time in Hildesheimer's
writing.

Blamberger interprets the "Häscher" material apolitically. Representations of vile deeds in *Tynset* and *Masante* are linked to the
Hitler regime and post-1945 restoration politics in West Germany
only to give the reader recent evidence that history repeats itself in
the form of men like the "Häscher." The narrator chooses passivity
as his response to these men, because there is no possibility of successful action against them (92).

Hanenberg points out that there is a new generation of pursuers
among the former Nazis, which makes their presence in society all
the more intimidating. Diethelm Fricke's birth date is 1928, so this
"Häscher" is somewhat too young to have been a Nazi (1989, 158;
see Hildesheimer 1973, 87; 1991a, 2, 202-3). In any event, "Häscher"
have no single history. They existed everywhere and always and
exist now. Since they are dehistoricized in *Masante*, the pursuers
function as elements of the plot rather than as involuntary and intrusive memories, and this is why the narrator can dismiss them
from his thoughts (1989, 160). It is a deceptive dismissal, because
just after he reports, "Die Häscher sind entlassen" (The pursuers
are dismissed; Hildesheimer 1973, 346; 1991a, 2, 349), he goes down-
stairs and is asked by the Irishman if he has his passport.

Hanenberg erroneously identifies this man as a police officer; the text is silent with regard to the man's official position, if he has one.

Alain is not present when the Irishman ("der Ire") requests the passport, adding that it is a mere formality (Hildesheimer 1973, 354; 1991a, 2, 353). Hanenberg names these two men as the narrator's pursuers, however – Alain merely because he remarked that the narrator would probably go out into the desert the next morning, since it was already dark (1973, 249; 1991a, 2, 294). Hanenberg decides that the narrator's disappearance in the desert is, on one level of comprehension, a reaction to the Irishman's request and Alain's prophetic statement. On another level, it is a response to the realization that history and fiction are useless. One cannot escape the pervasive repetitions of the same. The "Häscher" have appeared again, even after the narrator has traveled to the edge of a desert and dismissed them from his thoughts. The "Häscher" always win. The reality of horror always remains. History and fiction teach us nothing. The presence of "Häscher" at the desert inn proves that there is no escape from the continuity of horror even in so desolate a spot. It is for this reason that the narrator disappears into the desert (1989, 161-63).

Any reader of *Masante* will wonder who the Irishman is and why he wants to see the narrator's passport. The incident seems to be a variation of the narrator's story about Lüning (or Felber), who was approached by two men who wanted to see his passport. Later he thought these men were pursuing him (Hildesheimer 1973, 183-86; 1991a, 2, 256-58). Such a surmise might be Hanenberg's reason for deciding that Alain and the Irishman are the narrator's specific pursuers, but his reasoning lacks a textual foundation.

What no one has yet explored in *Masante* is why the man who asks about the passport is an Irishman. It should be noted that *Ire*, someone from "Irland," sounds like *irre*, a form of the verb *irren*, "to err." Neither Wetzel (1979) nor Rath (1985) has remarked on the sound correspondence in this instance, and in fact only Hanenberg mentions the Irishman.

Whatever significance this character has, it might have to do with the similarity between his nationality and the verb *irren*. Hildesheimer's penchant for wordplay comes into prominence some years later, in the *Mitteilungen an Max über den Stand der Dinge und anderes* (1981), but perhaps it is anticipated here. One might pursue the idea that the text is linguistically structured to show, on one level, the narrator's fear of pursuit even by an *Irishman*; but to hold out, on another level, the possibility of his realizing he could be *in error* and – by conquering his fear of pursuit – find his way back to the inn and eventually to Cal

Masante. The desert experience would thus enrich his life rather than end it. Both Wetzel and Andersson might agree with this supposition.

Goll-Bickmann, for whom *Masante* is a text of resignation and renunciation, would not. This critic too frequently interrupts the flow of his argument to insert quotations that prove again and again that the narrator has come to Meona to become creatively active. He could not write at Cal Masante, his Italian home, because the beauty surrounding him prevented concentration, and he did not have sufficient distance from his experiences. The narrator wants to make a new creative start here in the emptiness of his room, using the notes in his "Zettelkasten" (card catalog) and the stories he hears from Maxine. He fails, because the stories and reflections inspired by his notes and Maxine's monologues involuntarily recall his misery and intensify his melancholy, and he glides into dark realms of fantasy that come to an abysmal end (1989, 322-34).

Although Goll-Bickmann does not refer to *Tynset* in the body of his discussion of *Masante*, he states the basic difference between the two monologists in his conclusion. The *Tynset* narrator does not write, except for the name "Tynset," and he does not want to write. He exhibits a simple, nonpathological form of melancholy that is artistically productive, for with his pain come memories and images (360-61). The *Masante* narrator wants to write and is unsuccessful. He suffers doubly as he restrains the images that he creates. Even when his interior monologue furnishes a narrative and occasionally compensatory realization of images, he is frustrated in the end. His statement "Die Häscher sind entlassen" (Hildesheimer 1973, 346; 1991, 2, 349) is not to be understood as an autonomous act of dismissal, as if the narrator could make decisions about these pursuers. It is a confession of the conclusive breakdown of the pain mechanism mentioned when he said he was not worried about the end of life but about events accompanying the end (1973, 321; 1991a, 2, 334). As Goll-Bickmann reads this text, the narrator's experiences of failure with respect to the idea of becoming creative and in his relationship with Maxine cause a double melancholy (1989, 361). His argument is not thoroughly convincing. In fact, it seems contrived to fit what he – and many others – regard as narrative closure.

According to Jehle, *Tynset* and *Masante* share a thematic unity that Hildesheimer also expressed in collages between 1965 and 1971 (1990, 107-8). The major differences between the two monologues are formal. For one thing, *Masante* is based on collage technique, *Tynset* on musical principles. For another, the later narrator no longer tells his stories to himself, and they do not have the clear goal they had in *Tynset*. The dissonance that ensues between the narrator and Celestina in the earlier book is replaced by the consonance of the meetings between the narrator and Maxine, who is the same age as the narrator and whose presence diminishes him, a novel insight that Jehle elaborates as follows: because of Maxine, who is a grand figure ("eine großartige Figur"), the narrator is no longer exemplary or isolated. Her existence and survival make the narrator's end and the entire conception of *Masante* more inconsequential ("belangloser") than the *Tynset* narrator's decision to remain in bed (109-11). *Inconsequential* is an oddly disparaging term. The need for a comprehensive study of Maxine becomes all the more apparent with Jehle's evaluation of the second narrator in *Masante*, whom other critics describe as interesting, unusual, a mirror image of the narrator, perhaps a second absurd "I," but hardly a "grand" figure.

Jehle takes issue with the view expressed by Durzak and Hartlaub that *Masante* is more radical than the earlier book. He believes that the *Tynset* narrator could only reverse his decision to remain in bed if he came to distrust the conclusion he expresses during his monologue. The impetus for travel to Meona tacitly revokes the text of *Tynset*, but it presents no new conclusion. Jehle describes the later book as repetitive and a weak variation of the *Tynset* conclusion, therefore as actually confirming the text it revokes. If *Masante* had been written some years before *Tynset*, the narrator's decision to go into the desert would be more consequential than it is. Jehle cannot agree that the more drastic act in *Masante* produces a more drastic text (115). Neumann has much the same opinion in an article that deals mainly with *Marbot* (1986, 30).

Jehle's treatment of Maxine is especially remarkable for its brevity, in view of the fact that she is obviously the most important feature of the book for him. Because Jehle's opinions differ so dramatically from anything else written about *Masante*, they invite debate. His criticism emphasizes more than anything else the need for more study of *Masante*, including its structural and thematic relationship to *Tynset*. Jehle's reference to collage technique in the formal pattern of *Masante* might be further developed in conjunction and comparison with William S. Burroughs's discussion of his literary collage practices in the text, *The Third Mind* (1978), which he coauthored with the collagist Brion Gysin.

The only topic in both Hildesheimer books that seems to have been thoroughly researched is the narrator's melancholy mood. From the essays by Koebner, Nef, and Durzak in the 1970s to weightier discourse by Rath, Blamberger, and Goll-Bickmann in the 1980s, this aspect of Hildesheimer's writing – which includes the Hamlet motive – has been treated to extensive discussion. Blamberger even provides a survey of the concept of melancholy in prose from Homer to post-1945 novels in the first half of his book, as well as a chapter on psychoanalytical and sociological research on melancholy in the twentieth century (1985, 48-59).

Among the areas that deserve additional attention are the ramifications of introducing Maxine as a second narrator in what Blamberger convincingly identifies as literature of the absurd. It would be worthwhile to investigate the notion that the narrator is reflected in Maxine and decide whether she is indeed the split image of Lacanian psychology and what that means within the text itself. The writings of Herbert Blau, among others, might be useful in this connection, especially since both Petuchowski (1975) and Reichert (1987) discuss the theatricality of the text. Perhaps a psychoanalytical approach to *Masante* would be as fruitful as Blamberger's reading.

Much has been written about Hildesheimer's fascination with, and astonishing aural sensitivity to, the rightness of names in *Masante*, many of them introduced by means of the religious calendar (see Puknus 1978, 106; Lea 1979, 24; Wetzel 1979, 159). (Rath [1985] has nothing to say about these names, but he devotes a considerable amount of attention to the sounds and significance of names in *Tynset*.) Wetzel says that the saints' names on the calendar are indicative of occidental order (161), but Kurz, who moves the inquiry from names to issues they may represent, merely wonders why the narrator is interested in saints (1975, 74). Since nearly all critics agree that the narrator of *Tynset* and *Masante* is the same person, since the narrator of the earlier book makes it abundantly clear that he is a nonbeliever in Christianity, and since critics also agree that the narrator is a Jew, it is surely more than a little surprising that this narrator tacks a Christian religious calendar to the wall of his room at the hotel – especially since he values the whiteness of the walls in his room (see Goll-Bickmann 1989, 327). Stanley addresses the religious issue to some extent (1994), and Goll-Bickmann studies the narrator's godlike roles, but this aspect of Hildesheimer's writing has not yet been fully investigated.

Several critics respond to Wapnewski's term *poetische Enzyklopädie* and admire the narrator's wide-ranging knowledge (see Dücker 1976, 99). Perhaps the very realization of his intellectual prowess is intimidating, for scholars have yet to investigate the complex ideas in much of Hildesheimer's writing.

D. Poetry

Hildesheimer wrote fewer than two dozen poems between 1939 and 1984. They were originally published by the Fränkische Bibliophilengesellschaft in 1984 in a limited edition that included several full-color collages. The poems are reproduced in Volume 7 of the *Gesammelte Werke* (1991a, 545-56). Jehle, who edited the 1984 publication, includes a short "Nachwort" (afterword) in which he points out the author's use of quotations and wordplay in the poems, many of which deal with death, either as a concept or in specific terms (in memorials to Eich and Marilyn Monroe, for example; see 553 and 549, respectively). Jehle does not discuss the poems in *Werkgeschichte,* although he might have referred to them to support his observation that Hildesheimer was preoccupied with thoughts of death after he wrote *Tynset* (1990, 338-39).

The writer's own literary texts sometimes inspire poems. A tribute to Mary Stuart's acceptance of death, dated 1974 ("Mary Stuart," 1991a, 7, 554), is one example. Another, even more indicative of the writer's ability to distance himself from his writing and comment on it, was apparently inspired by the dialogue near the end of the radio play *Hauskauf* (House Purchase, 1974). Speaker A describes Saturn as "Anführer der Nacht" (leader of the night), to which Speaker B responds, "Dichter!" (poet; see 1991a, 5, 444). The poem "Leb wohl, Saturn" (Farewell, Saturn), which was written sometime in 1978 (1991a, 7, 555), is centered on a variation of Speaker A's metaphor.

The poems, like the fragments in *Nachlese* (Addendum, 1991a, 1, 457-88), the "Paralipomena und Materialien" (Additional Material and Notes) included in each volume of the *Gesammelte Werke,* and a large number of very short miscellaneous and aphoristic pieces in Volume 7 (513-43, 559-645, 649-711, respectively), will yield unexpected insights as researchers avail themselves of textual material that was formerly in limited circulation.

3: Nonfictional Texts

A. *Zeiten in Cornwall*

THOSE WHO DO NOT read editorial commentary on the inside cover of a book will not know that *Zeiten in Cornwall* is an autobiography. There is no textual indication that this Hildesheimer "I" is the author. Goll-Bickmann ignores the issue of nonfictionality in his structuralistic interpretation (see below), but all other critics comment on the identity of the "I." The most unusual response to the book's framework is that of Marcel Reich-Ranicki. He reviewed the book for *Die Zeit* in the summer of 1971 soon after its publication.

Reich-Ranicki notices a certain sterility in Hildesheimer's seeming preference for brilliance over substance. The writer gives the reader clever observations, literary allusions, a masterfully composed description of a fox hunt, and general reflections, but he avoids the personal confessions that one anticipates in even a partial life story. For example, Hildesheimer refers to labyrinth and maze images and describes himself as one who has gone astray, but he does not elaborate. It is, of course, a person's prerogative not to expose his errors to public judgment but when the writer of an autobiography alludes to some such matter and then changes the subject, he may deservedly be called coquettish. Reich-Ranicki wants Hildesheimer to shed more light on the dark areas of his life. Instead, we must content ourselves with only the briefest of information, and the narrator's discourse, as a result, resembles the performance of a striptease dancer who cannot overcome her bashfulness and strip (244-47) – surely one of the more colorful tropes in the history of literary criticism.

Like Hildesheimer, Reich-Ranicki left Germany in the 1930s, but in his case it was a forced departure. Of partly Jewish ancestry, he was deported with his parents from Berlin to Poland in 1938, and until 1943 he lived in the Warsaw ghetto ("Spiegel Gespräch," 1989, 140). As the reviewer of a memoir by a fellow Jew, who also spent the war years outside Germany, he objects to the narrator's failure to explain why he felt no sense of homelessness when he lived in Cornwall. The caustic "Sehr interessant" is an expression, no doubt, of the reviewer's incredulity and disappointment. The "very interesting" is very uninteresting because it is so unenlightening. Reich-Ranicki feels cheated, in fact, by a close-mouthed autobiographer, who does not even tell us when he lived in

Cornwall (Reich-Ranicki 1989, 246). Reich-Ranicki admitted later that his criticism was based on a preference for literature that confronts the present, and his "combative personal perspective" as a journalistic critic of literature in the 1950s and 1960s is well known ("Spiegel Gespräch," 1989, 140; Zimmermann 1988, 400-1); even so, his disappointment in the work would be acceptable if it were a traditional autobiography. It is not.

The editors of the *Gesammelte Werke,* apparently in consultation with the author, inserted *Zeiten in Cornwall* in Volume 1, "Erzählende Prosa" (Narrative Prose), which denies it status as nonfiction in spite of evidence to the contrary (see Durzak 1976, 282, where Hildesheimer says that the book is true from beginning to end). That there is no volume of autobiographical writing in the collected edition reflects Hildesheimer's frequent disclaimers about his narrative "I" (for example, in the Rodewald interview, 1971, 155). However researchers wish to deal with the applicability of the term *autobiography* in relation to any of Hildesheimer's writings, the editors of the *Gesammelte Werke* are inconsistent in their labeling of the several first-person texts. *Zeiten in Cornwall* and *Vergebliche Aufzeichnungen* are included in Volume 1, along with *Lieblose Legenden* and the novel *Paradies der falschen Vögel.* *Tynset* and *Masante,* which are related to *Vergebliche Aufzeichnungen* as reflective monologues, occupy Volume 2, "Monologische Prosa." Perhaps space considerations dictated that three texts be added to the narrative prose volume that do not really belong there (*Mitteilungen an Max über den Stand der Dinge und anderes* is the other).

Relatively little was written about *Zeiten in Cornwall* in the 1970s, as Jehle's *Bibliographie* reveals (1984, 182-83), although Koebner (1971) and Dücker (1976) mention the text in their thematic studies. When Jehle edited his collection of representative critical essays (1989) he chose to include the Reich-Ranicki review and a piece by Elisabeth Plessen that deals only with a portion of the text published separately in 1968 under the title "Fuchs in Cornwall" (Fox in Cornwall) in a collection of travel pieces edited by Heinz Piontek. Jehle seems to want to feature the most disparate viewpoints on *Zeiten in Cornwall,* because Plessen describes the excerpt as literature of the absurd (1989, 251).

Jehle tells us in *Werkgeschichte* (1990, 122) that Plessen explains the centrality of the fox-hunt description to the theme of the book and thereby contradicts Reich-Ranicki's statement that the fox hunt has no bearing on the autobiography (Reich-Ranicki 1989, 247-48). What Plessen discusses, however, is labyrinth imagery and its alienating effect on the reader (1989, 250-55). It is Jehle's opinion, then, and not Plessen's, that the fox hunt embodies the author's theme, which – according to Jehle – is that it is useless to go in search of one's own biography. The search will end in melancholy, for one does not conquer the past (1990, 125).

Zeiten in Cornwall is not an autobiography of personal details, Jehle writes, as he defends the work against Reich-Ranicki's review, but an investigation of the writer's beginnings as an artist in which the presence of the remembering "I" is always included. This "I" does not focus on specific objects, as it did in another preliminary text (in English), "Cornwall Interlude," published in the *Palestine Post* in April 1945. Instead it generalizes the past and distributes authorial comments among the various figures of the text or localizes them in Anthony, who at times becomes a self-portrait of the young Hildesheimer (115-23).

Another feature of what Jehle calls a fictive autobiography is the surprising presence of Maxine, who tells a story and then disappears (Hildesheimer 1991a, 1, 370-71; Jehle 1990, 123). *Masante,* of course, was not available to the public in 1971, but the radio play *Maxine* had aired in 1969. Surprisingly, Reich-Ranicki does not question the presence of this fictional character in the autobiography. It could be an editing error that was never corrected, but more likely Maxine's cameo role is another instance of Hildesheimer's penchant for blurring the distinction between fiction and nonfiction by "testing the limits ... transgressing and reversing an order that it accepts and manipulates" (Foucault 1977, 116). Jehle notes what might be another such blurring when the narrator mentions Queen Mary's hat, a topic that might have been carried over from the *Masante* work-in-progress (Hildesheimer 1991a, 1, 377; 1973, 202; 1991a, 2, 267; Jehle 1990, 123).

The limitless powers that the narrator exhibits with this stylistic technique are comparable to the tactics of a nineteenth-century omniscient narrator who stops the progress of the plot to make an aside. Goll-Bickmann fails to notice in his brief discussion of *Zeiten in Cornwall* that the appearance of Maxine represents a continuation or variation of the godlike characteristics he had earlier located in the *Tynset* narrator (1989, 262-90). The blurring effect of Maxine's presence would be worth investigating in connection with Hildesheimer's opinions on biographical and historical writing in the "Anmerkungen" (Remarks) to his play *Mary Stuart,* which premiered in 1970 but was published in 1971.

The reflecting "I" knows at the beginning of his reflections that his effort is doomed to failure. Jehle quotes (126) from a comment Hildesheimer made to Rodewald that the narrator's failure as a painter in Cornwall represents the writer's failure in all his artistic activities, including *Zeiten in Cornwall* (Rodewald 1971b, 142-43). The text itself, however, does not exhibit such pessimism, according to most other critics. They note a positive tone and satisfactory closure where Jehle reads flight from unresolved memories (127). There is no mention of flight or escape in the book itself. In fact, the narrator describes his mood at the end as one of relief: "ohne Wehmut oder Bedauern, eher mit einem Gefühl der Erleichterung" (without pain or regret, more with a feeling of relief; Hildesheimer 1991a, 1, 406). Jehle's determination that this leave-taking is flight is a distortion of the words that appear in the text and appears to be an attempt to connect *Zeiten in Cornwall* with the earlier *Vergebliche Aufzeichnungen*, where the narrator abandons the beach after realizing that there is nothing there for him.

Jehle attempts another – but much more likely – connection when he writes that all of Hildesheimer's work after "Schläferung" and *Vergebliche Aufzeichnungen* is an argument in which the author attempts to say what cannot be said, in a deliberate contradiction to the philosopher Ludwig Wittgenstein's statement that one must remain silent when confronted by the unsayable (127-28). It may be an unexpressed goal of Jehle's book to encourage new research by giving us hints of interpretive possibilities and novel approaches to reading Hildesheimer, because Jehle does not pursue the philosophical connection – or, indeed, any of the ideas he offers in a sort of pastiche fashion.

Puknus states the reverse of Jehle's comment: that the narrator realizes writing cannot re-create the reality of a past experience (1978, 98). Puknus is also influenced by the Rodewald interview of 1971, but he bases his interpretation of the text on the comment, "*Cornwall* ist ein Werkstattbericht" (*Cornwall* is a workroom report) and the related information, "das Ich denkt handwerklich im *Cornwall*-Text" (the "I" thinks in a workmanlike way in the *Cornwall* text; Rodewald 1971b, 142). The narrator's memories do not emphasize the horror of historical events taking place in Europe (as Reich-Ranicki expected) but offer an "Evidenzerlebnis" (a very clear presentation of an experience; 1978, 95). The speaker re-experiences the frustration he felt on his first visit to Cornwall as a student and his second visit after 1945. Puknus reminds us that it is also true that, far from being a failure as an artist, Hildesheimer actively pursued an art career in the mid1960s and even illustrated both *Zeiten in Cornwall* and *Vergebliche Aufzeichnungen*. What the writer writes about is thus not necessarily (as Jehle believes) a present or continuing failure. It is, rather, a coming-to-terms with the past ("Bewältigung"), completely unsentimental and not entirely positive (97-98).

No one has yet pursued the notion that *Zeiten in Cornwall* is, as the Puknus terminology would seem to imply, a text of

"Vergangenheitsbewältigung," the name given to anti-fascist literature in the GDR in the 1950s and especially in the 1970s but defined more loosely in West Germany as a postwar "mastering of the past" (Silberman 1987, 536). Critics other than Puknus report that the narrator satisfactorily masters a part of his past, and when their findings are added to Hanenberg's historically oriented interpretation (1989), there is a case to be made for including this work in the postwar genre (see Koebner 1971, 52; Dücker 1976, 98).

Zeiten in Cornwall contains only brief historical remarks, Hanenberg writes, because Hildesheimer had no reason to fear the Nazis when he was in Cornwall. He was safe from the horror of the Holocaust until he became a translator at the Nuremberg War Crimes Trials. He writes with restrained language about his own experiences during the period 1933 to 1945 because he did not witness the cruel reality of life as an exile. He was, instead, beginning his art career. As he himself said in an interview from which Hanenberg quotes, the war years were an interesting time in his life. And yet, superimposed on his memories of the relative happiness of that time are personal experiences in Israel, Nuremberg, and Germany. Hanenberg decides that Hildesheimer's only autobiographical text retreats behind observations and surrealistic fictions in order to master the times he spent in Cornwall as well as the uselessness, from a historical perspective, of reconstructing those times, for he could only touch on their terrors (1989, 151-52). The reason Reich-Ranicki was dissatisfied with the book has to do with its restrained language, which combines fiction and reality with literary and historical characters as it copes with memories of the past (146). The landscape of Cornwall, for example, reminds the narrator initially of the fool in *King Lear*. Associatively, he recalls an actor who once played the fool and who committed suicide during the war and Beckett's Vladimir and Estragon, who wait in vain for Godot (see also Plessen 1989, 253).

Fear, apprehension, and flight through suicide are encased in these memories but are not stated. The narrator's veiled reference to the gas chambers of concentration camps is one example of a restrained remark. Driving through a town, he accelerates: "ich gebe Gas," (literally, I give gas), and he adds, "ekelhafter Ausdruck!" (disgusting expression; Hildesheimer 1991a, 1, 351). In another place he uses the term "Nazimörder" (Nazi murderer; 1991a, 1, 364), but generally his expressions of fear or fright are allusive. All his disclosures are brief and obscured by artistic, surrealistic imagery, a characteristic that links this narrator to his *Tynset* counterpart (Hanenberg 1989, 149). Lea would most certainly not agree that the narrator masters the past. He finds a persecution motive in the gas chamber allusion as well as in the fox-hunt episode and the labyrinth imagery (Lea 1989, 53-54).

Hanenberg's description of restrained language and Goll-Bickmann's introduction of the phrase "Sprache der Melancholie" direct attention to Hildesheimer's language more usefully than Rath (1985) or the earlier critics, who – following Wapnewski (1973) – usually only comment on the erudition of the texts. It may be that Hildesheimer's learned and discreetly allusive language cloaks the sort of "Bewältigung" that occurs here in a text whose narrator was not in Germany during the war years but is nevertheless affected by what happened. In any event, it is apt to be a problematical addition to the genre, if indeed it qualifies for inclusion among works such as Christa Wolf's *Kindheitsmuster* (translated as *Patterns of Childhood*, 1976).

Reich-Ranicki's is the only voice raised in complaint about the lack of information Hildesheimer gives, and Jehle's is the only negative interpretation of the book. These are extreme views. For the most part, critics acknowledge the autobiographical nature of the text and locate its positive aspects. Dücker, for example, points out that the labyrinth motive loses its frightening quality and its literary potency as a symbol of hiding. The narrator realizes that he was indulging in wishful thinking when he regarded the bird as the embodiment of escape from reality, for it is dependent on others just as he is. His altered view of two important motives reveals the absurd quality of the narrator's prior alternatives to reality and his newly positive outlook at the end of the text (1976, 99).

The most useful discussion of the recurring bird imagery after Dücker is that by Goll-Bickmann, who identifies its bipolar structure. At first the narrator's observations about various birds have a melancholy tone, but he consciously invalidates it. The narrating "I" corrects itself and destroys the melancholy moment in favor of insight into the very prosaic condition of the object (1989, 374-77). The narrating "I" is a model of bipolarity in itself, displaying both resignation and affirmation of life and time. Because he can see the narrow inner framework of melancholy as well as the broader but neutral and unfalsified reality of things, the narrator is capable of letting go of his past history (378-79). It is not he, in this instance, but his companions of the past, Hal, Dennis, and Anthony, who exhibit melancholy. The narrator identifies with each of them and especially with Anthony, a thoroughly frustrated graphic artist, but he maintains a critical and often mocking distance from them as he objectively describes their situations (364-68).

Goll-Bickmann's investigation encompasses what he calls Hildesheimer's early and middle prose, and it contains a number of worthwhile revelations, among them the binary oppositions noted above. At the same time, by including *Zeiten in Cornwall* in his investigative plan, Goll-Bickmann confuses issues. First of all, he does not acknowledge that the text is autobiographical. He says only that the book is a reconstruction of the past at the conclusion of which the narrating "I" experiences a decidedly nonmelancholy feeling of relief (362). It makes no difference to Goll-Bickmann's structuralistic orientation that this text is reality-based; but it makes a great deal of difference to a reader of the Goll-Bickmann analysis, who is apt to assume that *Zeiten in Cornwall* is a work of fiction. The narrator's resolution of his melancholy is not as significant an act in a work of fiction as it is in an autobiography, which is read – like all nonfiction – with a different set of expectations. When the narrator is an artist, his discourse – in addition to satisfying our curiosity about the artistic process – can be instructive or even inspirational (Altick 1965, xi-xiii). Goll-Bickmann unintentionally diminishes the value of *Zeiten in Cornwall* by including it.

Second, Goll-Bickmann implies that there is late prose, but in actuality the only book-length text following *Masante* is *Mitteilungen an Max über den Stand der Dinge und anderes* (1983), the expanded version of a letter to Max Frisch that contains a number of allusions only Frisch could fully appreciate. It is therefore yet another reality-based text – like *Zeiten in Cornwall* – that blurs the distinction between fiction and nonfiction. The scope of Goll-Bickmann's book is thus as misleading as Volume 1 of the *Gesammelte Werke*, in which *Mitteilungen an Max* and *Zeiten in Cornwall* are included as fiction. He would have been better advised to eliminate *Zeiten in Cornwall* from his investigation and concentrate on purely fictional first-person narratives.

It is worth noting – and nearly every critic does – that Hildesheimer did not write another autobiographical account, although he readily admitted that he and his fictional "I" had characteristics in common. Because, as he said many times, he could only write from the perspective of a narrating "I," reviewers and critics, especially in Germany, have tended to consider all of his writing as autobiographical. It is perhaps because Hanenberg realizes how oversimplified such an observation is that he is not sure if *Zeiten in Cornwall* is really an autobiography (1989, 152).

In spite of the good work by Goll-Bickmann and Hanenberg, there is much that remains open to debate in *Zeiten in Cornwall*. It would be narratologically helpful, for example, to investigate the comment Hildesheimer made to Rodewald that his experiments with a manipulating "I" in this text were more important than the actual experiences he recorded (Rodewald 1971, 142). The blurring phenomenon with respect to the surprise appearance of Maxine also deserves attention. Jehle's reference to Wittgenstein should be pursued, as well as the notion that there might be enough of a conquest of the past and even "Bildung" to include this work in the genre of "Vergangenheitsbewältigung." Whether or not one agrees with Hanenberg that the radio plays *Das Opfer Helena* (translated as *The Sacrifice of Helen*) and *Turandot* are Hildesheimer's contribution to the genre (1989, 52-55), *Zeiten in Cornwall* deserves consideration in this respect.

The research described above can also contribute to general theoretical discourse about autobiographical writing and the various pitfalls and functions of an author, building on Foucault's essay "What Is an Author?" (1977) and investigations by Jacques Derrida (1976), who shares with Wittgenstein an interest in the limits of language.

B. *Mozart*

The cover and title page of *Mozart*, like those of *Tynset*, do not carry any designation of the book's genre. When it appeared in Germany in 1977 and in translation in the United States in 1982 it was placed in the biography section of bookstores and reviewed exclusively as a biography. In the essay "Die Subjektivität des Biographen" (The Subjectivity of the Biographer), included in *Das Ende der Fiktionen* (1984), however, Hildesheimer says that the designation is inappropriate (1984a, 123; 1991a, 3, 463). In a prepublication interview in 1976 he was more explicit: the book would be a monologue about Mozart if it were in first-person form; as it stands it is an essay, an attempt to make Mozart more accessible to the people of today (Kerle 1976; see Stanley 1988, 31-32). In another interview he contradicted himself and acknowledged that the text is indeed a biography, however unconventional it may be (Kesting 1986, 83).

Mozart appeared during a time of unusual biographical productivity in Germany. The 1970s saw the publication of at least a dozen biographies by such well-known writers as Christa Wolf, Adolf Muschg, Hans Magnus Enzensberger, and Günter de Bruyn (Beck 1986, 11; Neumann 1986, 22-23; Stanley 1988, 32; Jehle 1990, 137). If Hildesheimer was urged to complete his Mozart book by a publisher who wanted to take advantage of a trend, he did not begin the book because of it. He wrote several talks and essays between 1955 and 1966 before he decided to expand his study of the composer into a book (see Jehle 1990, 135-37).

The list of reviews and thematic studies of *Mozart* in Jehle's *Bibliographie* (1984, 191-207) is far from complete even to 1983, but it does indicate the quantity and variety of response to a book that was immediately regarded as controversial. In early reviews for the major newspapers and Sunday supplements, critics and musicologists commented – sometimes with admiration and sometimes with irritation – on the nonchronological, associative style of the book, the biographer's speculative and frequently mocking tone, his disinterest in sociocultural influences on the composer, and the generally unscientific nature of his research.

Musicologists argue about Hildesheimer's suppositions and cite factual errors, but in Germany his discussion of *Die Zauberflöte* (Mozart's last opera) proved to be so productively provocative that the bimonthly journal *Musik-Konzepte*, devoted one issue in 1985 to essays inspired by *Mozart*. Titled *Ist die Zauberflöte ein Machwerk?*, the issue includes a letter from Hildesheimer to Rainer Riehn, author of a lengthy article that questions a number of Hildesheimer's statements (Riehn 1985, 34-68; Hildesheimer's response follows, 69-75; the letter is included in Hildesheimer 1991a, 3, 440-48). Jehle reports that, beginning with the seventh edition of *Mozart*, factual errors found by Riehn and others were corrected (1990, 609, footnote 100). Riehn, however, is most interested in Hildesheimer's secondary sources and the conjectures he makes regarding authorship of the libretto. He objects especially to Hildesheimer's deemphasis on Freemasonry as impetus for the libretto and certain of his opinions about the characters in the opera. (See Stanley 1988, 59-61, for a summary of this argument.) Hildesheimer's response, in which he defends his opinions, may be of anecdotal interest to musicologists.

American musicologists were bluntly critical when the book appeared in translation. Marita P. McClymonds disputes Hildesheimer's statement that Mozart did not write program music and finds his judgments about Mozart's opera seria flawed by a "simple lack of homework" and by his inability to interpret the serious characters in either opera seria or the comic operas (1986, 278). Robert Craft complains that many of Hildesheimer's insights and judgments are unreliable or wrong. For example, Hildesheimer recognizes the value of such precocious marvels from Mozart's early years as the Piano Concerto, K. 271, but he does not seem to realize that "their emotional intensity is as great as that of almost any of the late music." Craft objects to Hildesheimer's undervaluation of *Die Zauberflöte*; he is surprised that the author failed to notice that the libretto contains ideas based on the French Revolution (1983, 130-31). Alan Tyson, a Mozart scholar who uses computers and beta radiology to fix the dates of manuscripts (he published a study of Mozart autograph scores in 1987), finds, in addition to dating errors, that all references to Beethoven "seem unduly faulty." He says, however, that the book "richly deserves to be debated" (1982, 7). And indeed it has been.

Discussion also centers on the type of biography Hildesheimer wrote and its goal. Among German scholars the text is regarded as a "literarische Biographie" because it relies on literary devices and may even be compared to the *nouveau roman* (Zeller 1980, 124-25; see Scheuer 1979, 209-47). American scholars use the terms *meta-biography* (Faber 1980) and *avant-garde biography* (Stanley 1988). Among the poststructuralistic readers of the text, Arens (1986) finds that Hildesheimer is only partially successful as a deconstructionist, and Hanenberg (1989) decides that the historical person is transformed into a literary figure. The more traditional interpreters, Puknus (1978) and Jehle (1990), stress biographical and psychological aspects of the text. Only one critic to date concentrates on the biographer's psychoanalytical stance (Weerdenburg 1986).

During Puknus's discussion of what he regards as the most important aspect of the book – Hildesheimer's lengthy pursuit of an answer to the mystery of Mozart – the reader might be reminded of Friedrich Schiller's essay on naive and sentimental poetry and a short story by Thomas Mann, "Schwere Stunde" (translated as "A Weary Hour"), in which an unidentified Schiller suffers late-night self-doubt as he works on the text of *Wallenstein*. The poet in Mann's story compares himself to his friend and creative colleague, Johann Wolfgang von Goethe (who is, of course, not named), and finally accepts the fact that his own gift is not inspired or naive, like Goethe's, but intellectual – that is, sentimental. With this acceptance of his individual talent and a glance at his peacefully sleeping family, the fictionalized Schiller returns to his desk (Mann 1975, 282-88). Hildesheimer resembles Schiller and Mozart is equivalent to Goethe in the Puknus reading of the biography. A writer's productive interest in a creative figure from the past can serve as a means of self-confirmation, Puknus writes, but that is not what happens here. When Hildesheimer returned to the theme of Mozart in the mid1970s, he began instead to work out a conflict between his ideal of art – a creativity that is simple, apparently unintentional, and pathos-free – and his own creative output, in which characters display pathos and a resigned passivity. The Mozart book reflects his acceptance of the difference between his own highly intellectual and self-conscious creative ability and Mozart's unself-conscious and therefore essentially pathos-free art (1978, 141-48). This unusual impressionistic view of the text is indicative of the variety of critical approaches to *Mozart*.

Apparently influenced by the commercial success of the book, the journal *Zeitwende* devoted an issue in 1979 to the theme "Wer war Mozart?" (Who Was Mozart?, the title of an earlier

Hildesheimer essay), but Gerhard Schmolze's "Mozart und die Religion" is the only article that specifically mentions the writer. Schmolze reviews the many conflicting opinions about Mozart's religious beliefs and the effect they had on his life and work. He agrees with Hildesheimer that the composer developed an expressive type of music that was somehow equally acceptable to the Catholic church and the Freemasons, but the issue of his religious conviction cannot be resolved, he decides (21-24).

The renewed interest in Mozart fostered among scholars by the Hildesheimer book spread to a more general audience after the appearance in November 1979 of Peter Shaffer's play *Amadeus*, the "single greatest success" of the National Theatre of Great Britain (Shaffer 1980, vii). The play became an acclaimed motion picture, garnering eight Oscars in Hollywood in March 1985. A useful summation of the popularization of Mozart in the media in Germany and Europe in the period 1977 to 1985 appears in the lead article of *Der Spiegel* for 16 September 1985, "Amadeus – das Ferkel, das Feuer speit" (Amadeus – The Scoundrel Who Spits Fire, 238-51). Its author, Klaus Umbach, describes Hildesheimer's book as a pre-Shaffer attempt to separate the man from the legend (249). Those who are familiar with Shaffer's play might notice that his Mozart resembles Hildesheimer's description, especially with respect to the composer's immature bursts of energy and humor.

Marion Faber, the translator of the book, describes *Mozart* as "meta-biography" because – in addition to being a biography – it challenges the content of former Mozart biographies and criticizes the method and practice of biography in general. All these aspects of the book are of equal importance, the translator says (1980, 203). Hildesheimer's goals are to establish the need for self-knowledge by a biographer and thus overcome the unwitting subjectivity to which biographers fall prey; to denationalize Mozart; and to expose romantic, idealized, sentimentalized, and misleading statements in biographies of the nineteenth and twentieth centuries. Hildesheimer's ultimate object is to counteract the mythologizing of Mozart that has taken place over time. He attains his goal by studying documents, employing graphology as an insight into character, and by referring to the psychoanalysis he himself underwent. As a biographer his advantage is that he is always conscious of his subjectivity. His technique generally resembles the Brechtian *Verfremdungseffekt* (alienation effect). "The machinery, the flies and wings of Hildesheimer's biographical stage are brightly lit" (208): Faber's concise description effectively counteracts the criticism of musicologists who object to the quality of Hildesheimer's research.

Stanley, too, speaks to the complaints of music critics when she explains that the author does not presume to be a scholar or to be authoritative. Actually, his book is meant for a reader like Hildesheimer himself, someone who reads music scores easily and "who listens to music both emotionally and intellectually" (1988, 36). Stanley's interpretation is the only large-scale effort in English. She explains early on that in English-language criticism "literary biography" identifies the biography of a literary person rather than (as in German criticism) the style of the writing (see Petrie 1981, 112-14; Stanley 1988, 32-34). She categorizes *Mozart avant-garde biography*, a term coined by Ina Schabert (1982).

The avant-garde biographer combines facts and novelistic techniques to construct rather than reconstruct the mind of the biographee. Discourse is candid in such biographies, which can "yield a certain Boffinesque charm as strange, unsettling reading experiences" (Schabert 1982, 13). Sartre's biographies of Genet, Flaubert, and Baudelaire as well as Richard Ellmann's *James Joyce,* Norman Mailer's *Marilyn,* and Hildesheimer's *Mozart* are the avant-garde biographies Schabert includes in her essay. Stanley adds to the attributes of this designation a didactic intention that she finds in the Sartre and Hildesheimer texts (1988, 6-7). As she applies the Schabert term, then, it subsumes the qualities of literary biography (in German and English-language critical discourse) and metabiography.

Stanley's chapter on *Mozart* takes a reader-response approach to the text, and she acknowledges that the reader may be irritated when the biographer uses the "we" form in his music analyses and opinions about various operas. Hildesheimer wants a response, however, even if it is irritation. He wants us to test our image of Mozart against that of the biographer and be "willing to accept a revised image" (65).

Hildesheimer's preoccupation with Mozart over the years, Stanley says, is founded on his realization that the composer "endured an absurd life with the aplomb Hildesheimer finds essential to survival in the absurd" (65) – a viewpoint shared by Jehle (1990, 141). Stanley compares Mozart's irresponsible behavior to the outbursts of Hildesheimer fictional characters who can no longer endure social constraints. The protagonist of "Das Atelierfest," for example, hammers a hole in the wall and escapes from his apartment to that of his neighbors; Adrian Walser in the play *Herrn Walsers Raben* (Mr. Walser's Ravens), transforms his bothersome relatives into birds.

The absurdist confides in no one, and neither did Mozart, as Hildesheimer's biography tells us. The absurdist does not express self-pity or despair, and neither did Mozart, with the possible exception of a letter to Da Ponte.

Hildesheimer accomplishes two didactic purposes in his study of this composer. First, he shows that even a musical genius cannot overcome the absurd, "although he may free himself from it intellectually for the period of time in which he composes and then performs music." Second, he reminds those who join him in his speculations that "music offers a listener the same freedom from the absurd" (Stanley 1988, 67-69).

In Katherine Arens's view, Hildesheimer is "attempting to deconstruct the various facades of pseudo-meaning that have been erected around the sign Mozart," so that he can see the "breadth of interpretation to which this sign can be subjected." His goal is to "reveal the scope of the ontology posited behind the trivialized facades" (1986, 153-54). Hildesheimer acknowledges that Mozart was a genius and instead of deconstructing the concept of genius he assumes its existence. By confronting an extensive array of biographical contradictions, he shows how genius "generates a series of conflicts"; for example, Mozart was supposed to be poor, but he had table silver until near the end of his life. If he was, however, poor and starving, how was he able to compose until his death? His highlighting of these and other contradictory statements in Mozart biographies constitutes "Hildesheimer's deconstruction of the stereotypes around the sign Mozart." The Hildesheimer book is "a sign whose presence pleads for the reader's acceptance of individuality" (157), but the text lacks historical and social dimensions. Hildesheimer does not address the issue of the individual as "a social necessity who can initiate change," and Arens includes in this criticism Hildesheimer himself in his role as a biographer. His failure, she writes, reflects a postwar German assumption "that modern society is bankrupt and cannot serve or encompass the historical veracity of the individual" (167).

The criticism is new only in its theoretical setting. Craft (1983, 131), Joachim Kaiser (1989, 286), Joachim Fest (1989, 292), among others, also complain of Hildesheimer's failure to include more than a vague image of the social and cultural background of the composer's life and works. Even Hanenberg, who finds historical significance in other Hildesheimer works, decides that the Mozart in *Mozart* is more literary than historical (1989, 195).

Arens's goal is to show the mutation of the cultural sign Mozart within three meaning systems: Eduard Mörike's 1855 novella *Mozart auf der Reise nach Prag* (translated as *Mozart's Journey from Vienna to Prague*), the Hildesheimer book, and Shaffer's play. Her conclusion that Hildesheimer, like his contemporaries in Gruppe 47, celebrates the potential of the individual instead of analyzing larger cultural or historical patterns betrays the inadequacy of her background investigation of the writer and his fictional – particularly his reflective – texts. Had she read any of the latter, she would not have written that Hildesheimer tends to "overlook the explicit history of the immediate past" (1986, 152). If she had read the essays on the absurd or the notes appended to the play *Mary Stuart*, she would have been less inclined to compare him to Böll and Grass.

Hanenberg's discussion intersects now and then with Arens's deconstructionistic view, as each critic deals with Hildesheimer's exclusion of cultural considerations in the biography. Hanenberg's conclusions carry more weight because of his greater knowledge of German (literary) history and Hildesheimer, but Arens at the very least compels us to look at this text from a poststructuralistic, that is, no longer parochial, perspective.

Hanenberg regards *Mozart* as a "literarische Biographie" because of the associational style of its discourse and references to the composer's "Rätselhaftigkeit" (impenetrability), which link *Mozart* stylistically to the fictional *Tynset* as a puzzle ("Rätsel"). Indeed, the puzzle of Mozart, whose frustration resembles that of the *Tynset* narrator, contains a number of particularities that will remind the reader of other Hildesheimer texts. Hanenberg mentions some of the same characteristics that, for Stanley, indicate Hildesheimer's recognition that Mozart endured an absurd life. Hanenberg's view is that the author takes the opportunity to work out, through this historical person, his negative view of historical events (explicated in the "Anmerkungen" to *Mary Stuart*) and his doubt that history has anything to pass on to us (1989, 192-95).

Neumann is intrigued by the fact that Hildesheimer actually contributed to the phenomenon of biographical writing in the 1970s, considering his antibiographical stance (1986, 23).

To Hildesheimer's disappointment, critics showed little interest in the significance of psychoanalysis for *Mozart* (Weerdenburg 1986, 63). His "psychologizing" (Craft 1983, 130) was not taken seriously in the United States, where more than one reviewer found his Freudian references and psychoanalytical assurances "tiresome" (Ekonomu 1982). Oscar van Weerdenburg's essay in the *text + kritik* issue of 1986 devoted to Hildesheimer is the only one that addresses the psychoanalytical foundation of the biography, and its conclusion is negative. Weerdenburg's essay will be most useful for those who are well read in Freudian psychoanalysis, understand the psychoanalytical approach to literature, and are familiar with the theories of Pieter C. Kuiper and Sebastian Goeppert, which Weerdenburg applies to the Mozart biography. Hildesheimer's biographical method deviates from premises of the psychoanalytical biography as defined by Kuiper in a 1984 essay in the following particulars: first, Hildesheimer does not determine how

Mozart's creative talent developed. He does not reveal, for example, a connection between the Bäsle letters and the *Requiem* that would show the relationship of productivity to the anal phase of development. Second, Hildesheimer attributes the composer's creativity to his unconscious, where it grows independently of external circumstances. Since the resulting compositions have no symbolic meaning for Mozart's life, according to Hildesheimer, there would be no basis – according to Kuiper – for employing psychoanalytical patterns of significance in an interpretation of these compositions. Third, Hildesheimer overestimates the value of self-knowledge in a biographer, which Kuiper does not regard as a guarantee of objectivity (Weerdenburg 1986, 64-68).

Hildesheimer's biographical method somewhat resembles the work of Goeppert, whose pertinent text was published in 1980, for neither forces the object of study into a preconceived theory. Both believe in self-knowledge in the interpreter (biographer) as a means of controlling countertransference. The advantage of this control is that one can deal dispassionately with one's subject and come to insights while impartially criticizing former methods. The disadvantage would be that there is no way to integrate this method into former methods (67).

Despite his goal to remain objective and his promise to balance all representations of Mozart, Hildesheimer does not succeed. Goeppert does not succeed, either, in his promise to align his method with metapsychology (67). Weerdenburg is not sure that Goeppert's interpretations accord in any way with psychoanalysis, and he is pessimistic about the value of Hildesheimer's biography of Mozart. Because the composer is, according to the biographer, that absolutely unique phenomenon, a genius, he is by the same token placed beyond all points of reference and thus effectively abandoned ("verlassen") by Hildesheimer (68). There has been no challenge to this singular opinion of the effect of the writer's stated purpose in *Mozart*.

Jehle's thesis, equally unusual and radically different from all others, is that Hildesheimer reveals an unconscious identification with Mozart through his choice of the first-person plural form of address. On a conscious level the "we" is meant to indicate intellectual identification of the reader with the biographer, as Hildesheimer says in the introduction to the book (1977b, 9; 1991a, 3, 11-12). Jehle explores the several ramifications of the "we," one of which is his whimsical idea that the "we" is the "I" of Hildesheimer's fictional monologues, which does not wish to be alone in the present context. The reader, included now in the "we," is forced into the role of the absurd "I." Both the absurd "I" and Mozart experienced life's contradictions and the impossibility of finding answers (1990, 134-67; see also Stanley 1988, 65-69).

Jehle quotes a statement by Hildesheimer to the effect that while he shows reality in his fiction as if it were absurd, in actuality the absurd is reality (Durzak 1976, 290; Jehle 1990, 141). Hildesheimer's view of life, therefore, finds its most striking parallel in the life and work of Mozart, and it is no coincidence that he has been in Hildesheimer's thoughts since the mid1950s.

Jehle's claim that Hildesheimer unconsciously identifies with Mozart undermines the writer-biographer's deliberate assurances to the reader, in his introduction to the text, that he is not fixated on his subject and is clearly aware of the subjectivity of his remarks. Unlike other biographers, he implies, he is knowledgeable about psychoanalysis and understands how to regulate his relationship to, and identification with, his subject. Hildesheimer explains this position more fully in the essay "Die Subjektivität des Biographen" (The Subjectivity of the Biographer), originally a talk given in 1982, which should be read by anyone interested in point of view in *Mozart*. He elaborates in part as follows: because he himself successfully completed a course of psychoanalysis, he can objectify himself and see himself as a someone who has largely freed himself from preconceptions and affect and come closer to self-evaluation (1984a, 137; 1991a, 3, 474-75).

Jehle's own determination is that Mozart becomes a figure through which Hildesheimer can speak, now that he no longer has a narrative "I." He partly supports his theory by referring to a confession Hildesheimer made in 1973 to Dieter E. Zimmer that he was unable to write about other people: "Ich kann nur über mich schreiben" (I can only write about myself; Jehle 1990, 149). Jehle does not cite the source of the quoted material, but it is the interview listed in his *Bibliographie* (1984, 89), and the subject is not *Mozart* but *Masante*.

Jehle combines textual evidence with personal information to establish his point that Hildesheimer identifies with the composer. When he notes that the excursus on humor perfectly characterizes Hildesheimer himself (1977b, 124-25; 1991a, 3, 128-29), he means as author of *Lieblose Legenden* and other texts, and as biographer of the Mozart book (1990, 151), but when he comments on a basic difference between Mozart and Hildesheimer, he means the author as a person (see 152, and the matter of the well-thought-out intellectual reply that was not, according to the biographer, of any interest to Mozart but is, according to Jehle, characteristic of Wolfgang Hildesheimer).

Jehle connects Hildesheimer the writer and artist with Mozart the composer when he declares that both were at their best when a theme was given to them. As Hildesheimer's best he cites, among others, the story "Schläferung," which was inspired by a poem of Hans Magnus Enzensberger; the collages (made from already-prepared papers); and the Mozart book itself, which is, of course, based on the life of another person (153). When he connects the biographer's remarks about Mozart's increasing noncommunicativeness to Hildesheimer's retreat from writing (because he felt he was misunderstood, not because he was overlooked), Jehle refers again to the writer as a person (149-50). The implication, as one reads through these examples and several others, is that the Hildesheimer fictional "I" is the writer himself and that this "I" as a person, a misunderstood writer, and a graphic artist is incorporated into the "we" that identifies unconsciously with Mozart the person, composer, and true genius. The implication not only calls into question but effectively overwhelms the biographer's claim that he can regulate the degree of his identification with his subject. This interpretation of the book is as controversial as the book itself.

Readers of Jehle's book will be distracted, unfortunately, by some technical weaknesses that become most apparent in the present chapter. For one thing, there is no bibliography in this text of nearly 700 pages. For another, footnote citations are sometimes inadequate. A reader who wants to investigate an intriguing comment by Gernot Gruber has a problem that cannot be solved by checking either Jehle's *Bibliographie* of 1984 or the more recent bibliographies in Stanley, Hanenberg, or Goll-Bickmann, for neither Jehle's bibliography nor the latter critics mention Gruber. There is no way to tell whether the italicized title, *Mozart und die Nachwelt* (Mozart and the Afterworld), refers to an article or a book by Gruber (all titles are italicized) or when and where it was published (1990, 608-9, footnotes 96 and 100). References to a Frank A. Meyer, who apparently interviewed Hildesheimer, are equally irritating. Jehle does not give even the date of the conversation from which he quotes (see 136, 153). Omissions of this sort (and there are not many) should be corrected. The addition of a bibliography is imperative. Jehle's references cannot benefit scholarship if they cannot be located.

The diversity of interpretations and the conflicting opinions surrounding *Mozart* should have a stimulating effect on future research. Schabert's claim that the Hildesheimer biography has features in common with biographies by Sartre and Ellmann, Arens's deconstructionist approach, and Weerdenburg's pessimistic dissection of the psychoanalytical basis of the biographer's discourse effectively open this text – and by implication Hildesheimer's fictional and nonfictional oeuvre – to even more varied discussion. Dorrit Cohn's references to the identity of the biographer in an essay on *Marbot* may be useful in further examinations of Jehle's stance on this issue (1992, 301-19).

Another area that merits closer study is the musicality of the writer's prose style, which has been analyzed in *Tynset* but nowhere else (see Haas 1975; Stanley 1977, 1979a). There are numerous insubstantial comments by literary critics (Jehle, Hart-Nibbrig, Weiss, and Muschg, among others) regarding the musicality of *Mozart* and *Zeiten in Cornwall*, but no one has identified the stylistic and rhetorical devices that constitute Hildesheimer's nonfictional musicalization technique, what the effect of this technique is on the writing itself, and what effect the intertwining of art forms in nonfictional writing has on the reader. Such a multifaceted topic is of considerable aesthetic interest in general, and Hildesheimer's writing can be of considerable specific value because he has incorporated musical devices consistently, if subtly, in fiction and nonfiction alike. Jehle reports that as early as 1952 a reviewer of *Lieblose Legenden* wrote that he found "viel Mozart" (much Mozart) in those early stories. According to Jehle, Hildesheimer is considered "der 'Mozart der deutschen Literatur' " (the Mozart of German literature; 1990, 146). Most likely no contemporary German writer has resorted so often to musical means as Hildesheimer, but unsubstantiated phrases about his musicianship only beg the question.

C. *Marbot*

On 29 February 1980, one hundred fifty years more or less to the day after the presumed death of Sir Andrew Marbot, Hildesheimer published an article in *Die Zeit* summarizing the life of this English nobleman, who was not yet twenty-nine years old when he died somewhere near Urbino, Italy (his body was never found). The editorial comment under a reproduction of Delacroix's drawing of Sir Andrew reports that the article is a draft of the ideas in Hildesheimer's new book, *Marbot*, a "gefälschte(n) Biographie" (falsification of a biography) to be published in 1981. "Die Wahrheit der Unwahrheit" (The Truth of Untruth) is the title of Hildesheimer's article (1980, 17). With so much information available, Jehle feels that no one should accuse Hildesheimer of wanting to deceive his readers (1990, 173; see also Raddatz 1982, 58). Indeed, most early reviewers of the book in Germany informed the public that Sir Andrew never existed. Among their designations for the book are "fiktive Biographie" (Krättli 1982, 163), "Versteckspiel" (a novel disguised as a biography; Bergman 1981), and

"Konstruktion," a text in which reality, fiction, history, invention, biography, and narrative are undifferentiated (Kesting 1982).

The translation was published in England and America in 1983. Terms such as "false honesty" (Blau 1984, 21), "sleight-of-hand" (Simon 1983, 12) and "bogus biography" (Fitzlyon 1983, 22) appear in reviews. The style of the book resembles "the genre popularized by E. L. Doctorow and other contemporary novelists in which fact and fancy mingle effortlessly" (Hefner 1983). Exceptions to such evaluations are few, but they create an unusual reception history for the book.

Johannes Kleinstück, who reviewed *Marbot* as if it were the biography of a real person (1981), attracted the particular attention of other German critics, because he is the author of *Die Erfindung der Realität* (The Invention of Reality, published in 1980) and should have been able to recognize an invented reality (see Jehle 1990, 610, footnote 111). Kleinstück reports, instead, that he could not find Marbot's name in the *Encyclopedia Britannica* and applauds Hildesheimer for having discovered this forgotten art critic.

J. P. Stern tells us in his 1982 article for the *London Review of Books* that he unsuccessfully tried to find Marbot in another reference book, the *Dictionary of National Biography*. In a startling exhibition of imitative wit, he leads the reader to believe (almost) that he believes that Marbot once lived. Hildesheimer wrote to the editor of the *London Review of Books* to correct what he thought was Stern's mistaken belief in the reality of Marbot. Jehle reproduces the gist of the letter and the editor's dry assurance that Stern understood the concept of the book (1990, 610, footnote 111; Stern 1982, 3-7).

Peter Wapnewski, who takes issue with the date of Marbot's visit with Goethe (see also Beck 1986, 36-37), embroiders the fictivity of the biography in an essay for *Der Spiegel*. He claims that he visited Marbot Hall in Northumberland and heard in neighborhood pubs that Lady Catherine Marbot had once taken in and cared for a sickly but beautiful orphan child. When it died, the child was buried near the Marbots. He also heard the legend of a hermit in Treviso who spent his life examining paintings. When he died in 1864, someone found a dueling pistol with the initials A. M. among his belongings (1982, 109-12).

These reviews illustrate the scope of early responses to the book and probably constitute the reason why Hildesheimer felt he had to emphasize the seriousness of the biography. When he accepted the 1982 Literature Prize of the Bavarian Academy of Fine Arts, and in the talks, "Arbeitsprotokolle des Verfahrens Marbot" (Writing Plan for Marbot) and "Schopenhauer und Marbot," both texts included in *Das Ende der Fiktionen,* he made it clear that *Marbot* is not a joke ("Scherz") or a satire or a parody. Whoever places the book in any of these categories "hat den Ernst der Absicht ... nicht erfaßt, das Thema verkannt und das Buch mißverstanden" (did not grasp the seriousness of its intent, did not correctly recognize the theme and misunderstood the book; Hildesheimer 1984a, 141; see also 154-55; 1991a, 4, 256, 272).

Wapnewski's seemingly frivolous attempt to trivialize the book might be based on the fact that he was present at a gathering in 1978 where the proposed text was discussed (Jehle, 1990, 610, footnote 112). At that time Hildesheimer treated his new project as a "Scherz." He also commented ambiguously in an interview in 1981 that the book was "ein enormes Spiel, ein Artefakt. Es hat ein sehr starkes artifizielles Element" (an enormous game, an artifact. It has a very strongly artificial element; 1981a; see also Stanley 1988, 88). The writing project became completely serious ("todernst") at some later point (Kesting 1986, 85), but the term *Spiel* (game) often appears in reviews. Fritz Raddatz, for example, uses it when he describes the "Double-Twist" in *Marbot*. The book is an endlessly varied game with words ("Sprachspiel"). It is a "va-banque-Spiel" to the point of frustration or failure that allows the writer to deceive the reader as he explores the theme of art as threat and oppression (1982, 59). The game in *Marbot* is so serious that Raddatz employs a gambling term ("va banque") whose consequences are either immediate riches or loss of everything.

The relationship between Hildesheimer and his subject or between Hildesheimer and his biographer persona is important to most critics of *Marbot*, and particularly to Cohn (1992), but there was early on a certain amount of confusion surrounding the book. In a speech before the Schopenhauer Society of Frankfurt in 1982 the author confessed that for him Andrew is so real that at times he wished the "Kerl" (rascal) had never existed. He was not the inventor of this figure, he said, but his designated biographer (1984a, 157-58; 1991a, 4, 274). Jehle notes that Hildesheimer did not repeat this "voreilige Identifikation" (unconsidered identification; 1990, 177).

During an interview some time later, Hildesheimer gave examples of opinions on art and literature that he invented for the biographee that were entirely different from his own (Kesting 1986, 88). In the "Arbeitsprotokolle" essay he modifies his position and acknowledges that he is indeed both the biographer and the world-weary frustrated Andrew, but that he is not the Andrew who had an affair with his mother, for he only partly identifies with his hero (1984a, 148; 1991a, 4, 262).

Helmut Heißenbüttel, who is also a novelist, complains that Sir Andrew's writings sometimes sound exactly like Hildesheimer's writings and are therefore not original (1989, 305). Jehle responds to Heißenbüttel in *Werkgeschichte* by noting that there are indeed themes and key words from other texts, such as *Flucht* (flight), in *Marbot*. There is also at least one direct quotation from the Büchner Prize speech of 1966, later published as "Büchners Melancholie" (Jehle 1990, 193-95). Material from *Masante* relating to the incest theme also appears (see Beck 1986, 91-92). Hildesheimer talked about this book on radio and in newspaper interviews beginning as early as October 1977 (see Stanley 1988, 111, footnotes 3 and 6), and, in addition to the article in *Die Zeit* in 1980 that introduced Sir Andrew Marbot, he published three other articles in 1981 (see Jehle 1984, 39). Some confusion about the authenticity of Sir Andrew's opinions may thus be traced to this proliferation of prepublication texts, but that is only one aspect of a complicated issue that continues to attract attention more than a decade after the book's publication.

Ulrich Weisstein, one of several distinguished scholar-critics who are intrigued by the complexities of the work, makes reference to a number of similarities between Andrew's opinions and those of Hildesheimer and others. The young nobleman's rejection of music for art is not unlike Hildesheimer's views on art in an article published in 1980, "Was sagt Musik aus?" (What Does Music Explain?; see 1991a, 7, 170-82). Andrew's "proto-Expressionist aesthetic" is "practically ... a quotation from Section 5" of Wassily Kandinsky's 1911 text *Concerning the Spiritual in Art*. Weisstein does not infer plagiarism, of course; he describes how Andrew's aesthetic differs from Kandinsky's (1983, 31-32). A comment by Marbot about literature reminds Weisstein of Percy Lubbock's 1922 text *The Craft of Fiction* and the critical debates on point of view that began with its publication (34). Marbot, Weisstein wants us to realize, is not an original thinker but anticipates theories that have already been advanced and are therefore not revelations to those who, like Weisstein, are conversant with theoretical statements on art, music, literature, philosophy, and psychology. Gert Schiff, who deals only with Andrew's art criticism, also recognizes resemblances to other sources, including the nineteenth-century Romantics, but he finds original insights in Andrew's critical discourse, as well, and an emotionality that is out of the ordinary in the early nineteenth century (1983, 146-48).

Neither Weisstein nor Schiff uses the term *intertextuality* to distinguish the theoretical intertwinings they find, but this postmodern concept is otherwise applicable to *Marbot*, and Hans-Joachim Beck proves it, although he does not use this particular word in his psychoanalytical interpretation of 1986. He refers, instead, to "Überblendungen," a term from film theory that might be described as an overlapping succession of subliminal cuts, and thereby brings a visual type of intertextuality to bear on the text. Eykman's references to a double perspective in *Masante* anticipate Beck's "Überblendung" theory (see Eykman 1978, 319-30).

Beck reads the text as a novel whose basic structure is determined by graphic art. He does not mean the paintings that Andrew studies but the thematic patterns in the panels on the door of St. Bernward's Cathedral in Hildesheim (which is not mentioned in the text). The six chapters of *Marbot* repeat these themes, and in this way Hildesheimer makes his own name the coded structural formula of his novel. All influences of cultural history in the book acquire the character of a closed system because the Hildesheim cathedral door represents their integrating center (1986, 112). To substantiate his unusual claim, Beck takes us through a treasure-trove of literary, biographical, and artistic influences on the text that initiate "Überblendungen" so intricate that they are sometimes dizzying. In fact, Beck's book should be cross-referenced with Goethe studies and English and German Romanticism in order to be fully utilized.

Anyone who wants to interpret the novel must first find the cultural sediments in the hero's unconscious that produce the "Überblendung" effect. Beck does not mention the work of Roland Barthes in this connection, but what he writes about the phenomenon of cultural sediments resembles Barthes's references (in *The Pleasure of the Text*, 1975) to the plurality of texts that exists for each reader within certain modern texts. The sediments that Beck finds will not be found by every reader of *Marbot*, for one would have to be as familiar as Beck himself is with the biographies and works of a number of writers, of whom Goethe and Thomas Mann are only the best known.

Beck's reading of what constitutes the "perpetual interweaving" (Barthes 1975, 64) that goes on in this text is unparalleled. Other critics mention similarities between *Der Erwählte* and *Marbot* (see, for example, Bormann 1986, 81), and Jehle discusses the influence of Goethe and Schopenhauer (1990, 187-92), but Beck goes so far as to declare that *Marbot* could not have been written without the influence of *Der Erwählte* and Mann's other novels and essays, which in turn reflect the influence of Hartmann von Aue's *Gregorius* (1187-89), Novalis' *Heinrich von Ofterdingen* (1802), Goethe's *Wilhelm Meisters Lehrjahre* (1795-96), and the works of Freud, Schopenhauer, Wagner, Lord Byron, and Nietzsche (114). All these creative men were themselves influenced by myth and religious legend, the Old and New Testaments, and each other, which creates even more of an interweaving. Beck does not mention the borrowings from Hildesheimer's own works that

Heißenbüttel, Schiff, Weisstein, and others find or the references to Kandinsky and other twentieth-century theorists noted by Weisstein and Schiff. He does not comment at all, in fact, on what Andrew wrote.

Beck as psychoanalyst discerns that Andrew's biography is based on massive repressions (27). Neither the author of *Marbot* nor the biographer of Marbot nor Marbot himself is able to discover his repressive defense mechanisms. Manifested in this threefold failure is the secret identity of author, biographer, and hero and at the same time the psychological principle of mythic transposition, which was anticipated in one of the stories in *Lieblose Legenden*, "Ich schreibe kein Buch über Kafka," in which the narrator proposes to write a book about Golch, who wrote a book about Boswell, who wrote the biography of Dr. Samuel Johnson (116).

Andrew Marbot's biography is based on three structural levels that represent the hero's unconscious. On the mythic level Marbot personifies Hercules and Oedipus. In biblical terms he appears as the Old Testament Adam and personifies, by identifying with Christ, the New Testament Adam. On the historical-human plane Marbot represents, in mythic identification with August von Goethe and Lord Byron, the physical and spiritual son of Johann Wolfgang von Goethe. Goethe, in turn, as God-the-father and Jupiter in one, prevails as father figure of Marbot's superego. Andrew tries to bring to consciousness the myths represented in art and literature, but as he tries he falls prey to the compulsion to repeat these culturally transmitted myths unconsciously in his own biography and becomes in the end a mere model and a myth himself. The myth of Marbot encapsulates Greek and biblical myths and becomes a synonym for cultural history. By discovering the deep structure of the discourse, the interpreter will accomplish what Marbot would have had to accomplish to heal himself (115-19).

Beck believes that the biographical discourse of *Marbot* functions as a special kind of autobiography (which he compares with Mann's *Doktor Faustus*), and that Hildesheimer works out problems of his own psyche in his text. A fourth level of interpretation, Beck suggests, would be to develop the novel from the biography of the author (124-25).

Beck's interpretation is unique and in some respects controversial, if not downright fanciful, but it opens an extraordinary door (no pun intended) to Hildesheimer research. One concomitant of this interpretation is that Hildesheimer's often-expressed disinterest in literature as well as his habit of giving wrong or contradictory responses when asked about his literary background become not merely suspect but inexplicable (see Zimmer 1973; Durzak 1976, 273; Postma 1987, 221; Hildesheimer 1991a, 7, 747). Weisstein describes

Hildesheimer as a "veritable polymath" (1983, 36), and Beck's array of "Überblendungen," if one accepts them all, more than confirms the judgment. For whatever reason, however, the writer preferred not to discuss the development of the intellectual biography that lies below the surface of his writing (see Raddatz 1982, 59).

When he was interviewed by Kesting, Hildesheimer said that he had two goals in *Marbot,* both of them relating to art: to show that the Romantics and even Goethe viewed early art peculiarly, and simply to discuss art (1986, 86). Kesting did not ask about literary influences on the text, for literature itself plays only a small role in the book. Andrew is suspicious of literature, in fact. Weisstein surmises that this skepticism has to do with the notion that "words about words" resemble "rhetorical surfeit obscuring rather than revealing what is underneath" (1983, 33). Perhaps Hildesheimer's evasive and obviously inaccurate responses to questions about his literary background are reflected in Sir Andrew Marbot's attitude toward literature.

In an essay published the year before the Kesting interview, Käte Hamburger anticipates the writer's comment that he wrote *Marbot* in order to be able to discuss art. Like Weisstein and others, she finds the text unique but unsatisfying, and she has a thoughtful response for those who, like Heißenbüttel and Beck, claim that the text is a novel. It is *neither* fiction *nor* biography, she writes, because it includes real people who are not fictionalized along with fictional characters who are presented as real. It is thus not comparable to *Doktor Faustus,* as sometimes claimed, or to historical novels, but might be described as Hildesheimer's "dichtungstheoretische Paradoxie" (poetic theoretical paradox; 1985, 204). The biographer's claim that Marbot prefigures the theory of the libido, and all his other claims, lose their validity once the experienced reader realizes from the clues given that Sir Andrew – despite all pictorial evidence – is an invented figure. In the end the book is a record of the writer's opinions and interpretations of art, whether serious or parodistic or both, but given to an invented figure that is presented as a real person. Tilman Jens might agree in part with Hamburger, for he reads the book as a deeply serious game played at the edge of silence (1986, 1-7), a reference probably to Hildesheimer's remark that no one could write a second such book (see 1984a, 150; 1991a, 6, 264).

Those who read the text as fiction include Kesting, who advises us not to confuse the biographer with the author, for the former is too pedantic – like the narrator in *Der Erwählte,* which also deals with incest. Hildesheimer uses his invented biographer as a kind of straw man so that he, the author, can remain at a safe distance from his dangerous and seductive hero. In addition to emphasizing that *Marbot* is a novel, Kesting points out two aspects of the text that will be amplified in later investigations: there is a lack of daring in the art interpretations and ideas that Hildesheimer gives his invented figure; the incest material is presented in an unerotic manner that weakens the text (1982). Heißenbüttel repeats this latter comment in his discussion of the book as narrative fiction (1989, 302-4).

The unerotic quality of the incest material is essential to the text, according to Schiff, Stanley, and the most recent critics, Japp (1990) and Cohn (1992). Schiff compares Andrew's incestuous desire, which is shared by all of us but at the same time sharply tabooed, to the writer's wish to make his invention truth, for this wish, too, was tabooed when the gods ruled over earth, man, and demigods such as Prometheus, who was punished for enlightening man (1983, 149). Stanley modifies Schiff's insight by describing the incest as an objective correlative to what was regarded by the gods as the creative artist's demiurgic magical powers. To make Andrew plausible Hildesheimer gives him a passion (for his mother) that is equal in intensity to a writer's desire to create truth. Andrew sublimates his passion in his art investigations, once it becomes necessary to separate from his mother. When he realizes that he cannot reach into the soul of an artist, we accept the revelation as "real evidence" and the man as real because we appreciate the extent of his commitment to his work and his incestuous love (1988, 89). Japp and Cohn, in references to the Heißenbüttel review, point out that the biographer had to remain unimaginative with respect to the incest incident in order to maintain his objective stance (see Japp 1990, 222, which anticipates Cohn's discussion of nescience, 1992, 305-6; see below).

As a result of these interpretations, the Kesting and Heißenbüttel complaints about unerotic incest descriptions lose whatever impact they had. Jehle further undermines Heißenbüttel's review by quoting from the latter's novel *Ödipuskomplex Made in Germany* (1981) to show the tastelessness of Heißenbüttel's sense of the erotic (1990, 617, footnote 121).

Weisstein applauds *Marbot* as a "fascinating novel," but he pronounces it at the same time a "magnificent failure." The book's experimental and ambitious structure is fascinating; its content is a failure by reason of the many "inconsistencies in Marbot's still half-baked philosophy of art" (1983, 36), which is nothing but fragments of an "aesthetic confession loosely, and somewhat frantically, gathered in the final years of Marbot's life" (33). Hildesheimer cheats the reader by first withholding information and then causing his hero to die young. If, by withholding information, Hildesheimer meant "to tease us by whetting our appetite" for the future publication of Marbot's collected works (33), then the writer either sabotaged his own expressed wish to see dissertations written about Andrew by not providing such a scholarly edition (Stanley 1988, 76-77), or he deliberately created an unreliable narrator, which is the thrust of Stanley's interpretation.

The discourse of *Marbot* is didactic and, in the end, "about biography more than ... about Andrew Marbot" (80), Stanley says. The text is a mock-biography according to the definition given by Timothy Dow Adams and is similar in some ways to Virginia Woolf's *Orlando: A Biography* (1928) (8,75). Characteristics of this subgenre include "a false air of non-fiction," frequent disregard for chronology, inaccuracies of fact, the mocking of scholarly conventions, "flashes of truth," and emphasis on the supposed biographer (80-103).

Stanley's discussion is as unusual in *Marbot* criticism as Beck's, for she compares the book to English-language texts and focuses most of her attention on the last-named characteristic above. The biographer becomes a crucial figure in Part 6 when, after describing Andrew's disillusionment, he reveals by his failure to note his subject's ability as a writer "the power of literature to influence the reader to question what is presented and make an independent and contrary judgment" (106). The biographer is a professional writer, and a good one. An American art critic describes his discourse as a "masterpiece of chiaroscuro" (Blau 1984, 21). And yet he does not notice how well Andrew writes, although it is evident to the reader.

Stanley's explanation for the biographer's surprising omission is that he became so engrossed in the opportunity to talk about his own disillusionment with literature and language through his subject that he failed to acknowledge Andrew's effectiveness with words, "although it was those very words that most certainly attracted him to the subject in the first place." He thus exemplifies "the negative consequences of Freud's declaration that every biographer is fixated on his subject" (107). The reader must do some of the biographer's work to complete the biography, and our participation in the text allows this mock-biography to retain the instructive quality that is an aspect of traditional biography. For example, the reader learns that a biographer may not be able to tell the full story of his subject's external life for unconscious reasons, and he cannot tell the full story of a subject's inner life. Sir Andrew teaches us the second part of this truth, the biographer the first part, as he fails to discuss his subject's creative ability. The reader so instructed may become skeptical of biographical or documentary writing in general and also realize the truth that people "cannot really know one another or learn from another's mistakes, for we never fully reveal ourselves and our motivations" (108-9).

Hanenberg agrees that *Marbot* contributes to biographical – that is, historical – writing. Paradoxically, it acknowledges at the same time that it is a kind of fiction, a "Superfiktion" (Hanenberg 1989, 197; Stanley 1988, 108).

Neumann, who has followed Hildesheimer's literary career from its inception and on occasion advised him, contemplates the writer's contradictory stance as absurdist, outspoken critic of biography, pessimistic author of an essay proclaiming the end of fiction, and biographical writer in an essentially biographical study of *Marbot* that assumes that the reader is as knowledgeable as Neumann about Hildesheimer's writing. *Marbot*, Neumann writes, reveals the conquest of a crisis peculiar to literature of the absurd that manifested itself in *Masante* as creative stagnation, for the latter book only varies and repeats the material of *Tynset*. *Mozart*, whose absurd premise is the necessity of frustration, thematizes the crisis. In that biography Hildesheimer succeeded in showing the compromise between his will to understand and the absurd certainty that the most important of our insights will remain closed to us. *Mozart* is thus a joining of absurd philosophy and a Freudian hermeneutic (1986, 30).

The fictive Sir Andrew, who refuses to live with (absurd) frustration, resolves the issue by committing suicide. Neumann does not compare the suicide to Hildesheimer's decision to end his literary career after *Marbot*; but his conclusion implies the connection, because he regards Hildesheimer's identification with his subject as stronger in this fictive biography than in his first-person narratives, in spite of the distance the biographer maintains from Sir Andrew.

The fiction of this text is not simply that of an English nobleman but of the future in general, that is, a future in which educated people will talk about works of art. Since Hildesheimer believes that no such future is possible, he had to place his biographee in the distant past with a future that is a fact, for he wants his subject to talk about what is most important to him, namely art. In the distant past an invented Andrew can comment as if art were still part of a collective reality and had a future, for at that time it was, and it did (32). In a sense, Hildesheimer suspends his own disbelief and writes against his convictions, conquering for a time the crisis of a future-less life. Neumann's perceptive interpretation rounds off the insights in Blamberger's study of Hildesheimer as an absurdist (1985, 74-100).

Uwe Japp points out fictional signals in *Marbot* as he develops his theme that this text – by the author of a 1975 essay proclaiming

"The End of Fiction" – is a demonstration of innovative fictional writing that disputes the thesis of the essay, which is not, in any event, new. Japp reminds us that Aristotle, Hegel, and Nietzsche had each reported that literature had arrived at a point where further development of the art could not be expected (1990, 212-13).

Jehle devotes considerable space to explaining the seriousness and "souverän" (masterful) execution of the text. For example, almost forty paintings and more than fifty painters and architects are mentioned in *Marbot*, as well as sixty writers of literature and philosophy and approximately fifty of their works. The biographer and Marbot himself quote from Greek, Latin, Italian, French, German, Spanish, and English literature (1990, 180). This dry recitation of facts adds credence to Beck's detective work and all the more weight to Weisstein's and Beck's recognition of Hildesheimer as a polymath.

In his discussion of the themes of melancholy and flight, which are as pervasive in *Marbot* as they are in the reflective texts, Jehle's own writing mimics the spiraling movement ("Spiralbewegung") that he attributes to *Marbot* (202). The term *Spiralbewegung* might remind the reader of Friedrich Schlegel's concept of the literary arabesque as well as his formulation of "Universalpoesie," which Beck applies to *Marbot*. Beck also calls the book a realization of the Wagnerian idea of "Gesamtkunstwerk" (complete work of art), thereby shifting his emphasis back and forth between Early Romanticism in German literature and Romanticism in music and creating an independent interpretive "Spiralbewegung" (see Beck 1986, 123). Discourse about *Marbot* tends to provoke as elaborate a display of syntactical skill as one finds in the original text.

The biographer's pedantic tone indicates to Jehle that he is probably not an artist. He is sometimes ridiculous and far less reflective than the *Mozart* biographer, and he is not to be confused with Hildesheimer (1990, 176-83). Jehle is especially critical of Alexander von Bormann, who declares that Hildesheimer is the biographer and calls the text a novel with a theme that creates "fast ein Skandal" (nearly a scandal) for its superficial understanding of Freud and incest (1986, 76-82; Jehle 1990, 615, footnotes 115, 117; 616, footnote 119).

Jehle defends Hildesheimer's creativity more than once. The defense is unwarranted in every instance and interferes with the reader's appreciation of the writer's belief in his subject, which is not to be confused with author identification. There are, as already noted, borrowings from Hildesheimer in Andrew's notebooks, but one must accept as part of the "Superfiktion" of this text that, aside from those borrowings, what Andrew wrote is his own opinion. Conversely, whenever Hildesheimer quoted from Andrew's notebooks in talks and newspaper articles, he was quoting from Andrew. This situation is not a matter of identification with the subject but recognition of the creation as separate from the creator. Unfortunately, Jehle does not notice this belief system; instead, he says that Hildesheimer identifies extensively with both Marbot and Mozart (1990, 204).

Cohn, on the other hand, argues that Hildesheimer wants to be recognized as the biographer of both subjects and expects the reader of *Marbot* to recognize him as the biographer of *Mozart* based on intertextual recollections of the earlier text in the latter. Like Weisstein, Hamburger, Japp, and others she notes the indications of fictionality in the text (the illustrations are the most striking). She contradicts Japp's contention that the objectivity in *Marbot* is to be differentiated from that in *Mozart* (1990, 222) and supports her view by stressing a narratological situation that Hildesheimer did not take into account: the reader will exercise the option to separate the narrator from the author when it becomes clear that *Marbot* is fiction, in spite of the absence of narrative language and devices such as omniscience. As a result, the normative language of the text becomes ironic and even self-parodic (1992, 311-16; see also Hamburger 1985, 203).

Cohn describes *Marbot* as a postmodern historicized fictional biography, an inversion of such fictionalized historical biographies as Hermann Broch's *Der Tod des Vergil* (translated as *The Death of Virgil*, 1945), because the narrator does not allow himself to enter the mind of his subject or to include any data for which he has no documentary evidence. Nescient rather than omniscient, the narrator continually asserts his lack of knowledge and, even when he imagines the incest scene, maintains a bland, nonmimetic style of discourse. Cohn's essay reveals how important it is to pay attention to the ramifications of the author's choice of a normative rather than narrative mode of communication. This is a unique text, and it will likely remain unique, Cohn says, because the narrator's rigorous antiomniscient stance opposes the postmodern trend to open boundaries between fiction and fact (319).

The French translation of *Marbot* appeared in 1984. Jean-Marie Schaeffer responds to the text in 1989 in the second section of an essay that is a restatement of material in the Stanley, Hamburger, and Cohn interpretations. According to Schaeffer *Marbot* is the perfect simulation of a real biography. It is a serious sham: that is, it aims to create the illusion of a real biography, to usurp the position of biography; an artistic sham, on the other hand, wants to be recognized as illusion (1989, 119). While both Hamburger and Cohn might agree with Stanley that the text means to be accepted as a biography, Cohn declares that the reader will not accept it as other than fiction.

Hans Hartje comments that the pseudo-critique of false documents in *Marbot* is related to Woody Allen's pseudo-documentary film, *Zelig* (1990, 76). Real people (Saul Bellow and Susan Sontag, among others) describe their former friend, the invented Leonard Zelig, once celebrated for his ability to change his physical appearance in a chameleonlike manner. A comparative study of *Marbot* that included this film and E. L. Doctorow's *Ragtime* (book and film), as well as other works that combine reality with fiction, would be instructive. It would be at least equally valuable to compare the Hildesheimer biographer with probably the most famous of his invented colleagues, Charles Kinbote in Vladimir Nabokov's *Pale Fire* (1962) and Dr. Serenus Zeitblom in Mann's *Doktor Faustus* (1947).

Religion remains an inadequately explored thematic issue in Hildesheimer's nonfiction. It is an element of his conception of the absurd, according to Dücker (1976, 36), and it permeates the biographies. Even if one regards with some skepticism Beck's discovery of a cathedral door as the key to *Marbot's* structure (1986, 112), it is true that the tenets of Catholicism influence the lives this writer chose to depict in *Marbot* and *Mozart*.

Finally, a comparative study of the various reading strategies examined above, together with the Hamburger and Cohn discussions of the author's role in this inversely significant postmodern experiment, might facilitate interpretation of the fictional biographies and autobiographies, whether serious or artistic shams, that have been published since the trend to biographical writing began in the 1970s.

D. *Mitteilungen an Max über den Stand der Dinge und anderes*

Hildesheimer's last literary work, published in 1983, excited much laughter and imitation from reviewers. Willy Hochkeppel copies its convoluted hypotactic sentences in his review (1989, 327). Hellmut Seemann, like most reviewers, mimics rhetorical devices (1984). The text was translated into English by Joachim Neugroschel in 1987, but the idiomatic expressions that dot the work lose their potency in translation, and what is actually intertextual richness sometimes sounds downright silly in English. This is a text better left in the original. It is Hildesheimer's most private text in an oeuvre distinguished by its hermetic quality. Some references are so obscure that they seem intended only for the eyes of the original reader, Max Frisch. For the first time, Hildesheimer does not communicate to a cosmopolitan audience that would include his English-speaking readers.

The work is the final revision of a letter to Frisch, the Swiss novelist and playwright. The original was published in 1981 in a collection of essays honoring Frisch on his seventieth birthday. It was revised and enlarged that same year and read by Hildesheimer during a radio broadcast. Another version was published in 1982 in the journal *manuskripte*. An unauthorized and truncated version was also published before the present text – with illustrations by Hildesheimer – appeared (Jehle 1990, 204).

The writer mentions a dead friend but does not name him. Thomas Schneider explains that the reader who is well read and enjoys playing detective will recognize from a reference to "Lebus" that the friend is Günter Eich. Schneider finds thematic connections between the letter and Eich's *Maulwürfe* (Moles, 1968) and Frisch's *Der Mensch erscheint im Holozän* (translated as *Man in the Holocene*, 1979). Both Hildesheimer and Eich despair of the future, but rather than complain about the senselessness of acting against a relentless reality, they turn to encyclopedic sarcastic mockery. The allusive language of *Maulwürfe* and the absurdities of *Mitteilungen an Max* are equally esoteric. Frisch, too, plays word games, but the more important reason for Schneider's comparison of the Frisch and Hildesheimer books has to do with the protagonist's response to his situation in the Frisch book and a similarity of narrative technique and structure (1985, 357-61).

Geiser, the Frisch protagonist, refuses to open his door to the men who have come to rescue him following rock- and landslides in his village. He does not wish to return to society. Hildesheimer's book is a response to the intrusive knocking at Geiser's door that punctuates the last part of the Frisch text. The response is, as Schneider carefully examines its linguistic details, an acknowledgment that there is no possibility of changing the course of the world. Geiser may be senile by the end of his ordeal, but he calmly accepts the transitory nature of life. So does the letter writer, who knows that it is too late to avert or avoid destruction of the environment and the end of life as we know it (376-77).

The letter is not an autobiography, although it does not conceal its autobiographical origin. Hildesheimer mixes personal and general remarks, truth and lie, and fiction and reality in a montage of word games, idiomatic expressions, turns of phrase, and quotations (even from his own works) that disturb the confidentiality of his remarks and reveal the end of fiction (364-66).

Schneider also compares the text to Jürgen Becker's book, *Ränder* (Boundaries, 1968), for which Hildesheimer prepared a review that might hold the key to understanding *Mitteilungen an Max*. Hildesheimer describes Becker's associational chains of thought as a "Protokoll" consisting of expressions we all know from our own experiences. Becker's goal is to describe the act of writing in spite of its indescribability (see Hildesheimer 1991a, 7, 321-26). Hildesheimer might just as well have been reviewing Frisch's *Tagebücher*, published about the same time, Schneider observes, for Frisch's narrative objective is similar (1985, 365).

Frequent references to Middle High German in *Mitteilungen an Max* will alert the reader-as-detective to the significance of the Middle Ages. That was the period when the adage and the aphorism became prominent features of literature, which was written on parchment or papyrus that can be washed or scraped and subjected to sophisticated photographic methods to reveal a text (an "Urtext") underneath. Hildesheimer creates just such an "Urtext"-situation with his display of ambiguities meant to point out communication problems in the wake of the technical and industrial revolution and the atomization of society (373-75).

Hanenberg reads this text as a personal statement of Hildesheimer's inability as a writer of literature to have an effect on the course of social history, which is threatened by the spoilers of nature rather than fascists (1989, 208-9). Jehle describes some of the private jokes and stresses the personal tone of this final farewell to literary writing (1990, 204-12).

Stanley's position is that this didactic text can be a positive experience for the reader who participates in the fulfillment of the book's potential. Such a reader may feel a "renewed appreciation of the past and our cultural heritage." One may be jolted into protesting against "progress that corrupts rather than refines. The letter writer's resignation and his isolation" need not be our response to very real environmental dangers (1988, 143).

Readers are apt to relate differently to the numerous quotations, aphorisms, and word games in the text, as Jehle's objection to certain of Stanley's interpretations reveals (1990, 628-29, footnote 146). Since not every reader will have Jehle's access to the writer, any interpretation is apt not to coincide with biographical fact; but it need not be absolutely wrong, as Jehle seems to think. Each new and different reading may illustrate, rather, the capability of this work to stimulate thought. Jehle's determination about what Hildesheimer means by any of his word plays is always of interest, but it is not crucial to a reader's interpretation.

The text is, however, a most unusual addition to the Hildesheimer oeuvre. On one level it is a highly personal memorial to a friend in a letter to another friend, and on that level it should not be a public document. Its absurdities of language may be amusing to some readers, but its pessimism and the black humor that is not always in good taste can drive others away. The target audience for this text, since it has become a public document, is smaller than even the intended readership of *Marbot*, for at least some of the German adages will remain hidden from non-German readers. One might draw the inference that Hildesheimer wishes to exclude most readers from his farewell to literature. If that is the case, it is paradoxical that he decided to create a publication from his original letter and thus expose it to the scrutiny of strangers. Since there would be little point in antagonizing his audience with incomprehensible reading material, it is more likely that he hoped to challenge those who read his text to scrape the surface of his parchment and find an "Urtext" and by means of this intellectual game to find a way to cope with the end of life as we know it (Stanley 1988 123-43).

Schneider's identification of the influence of the Middle Ages on Hildesheimer's literary work supports Beck's identification of the early cultural sediments in *Marbot*. Hildesheimer shows us in the present text that he is familiar, too, with the work of early twentieth-century poets such as Rainer Maria Rilke, Stefan George, and Hugo von Hofmannsthal. It is true that he is not, like Jens or Neumann or Wapnewski or Weisstein (to name a few contemporaries), academically associated with literature, but that is the only context in which he might justifiably have claimed that he had nothing to do with literature (see Zimmer 1973). His knowledge of and familiarity with a broad base of German and English literature and philosophy are, in fact, as inspirational to a reader as the messages one may find in his writing.

E. *Nachlese*

Mitteilungen an Max is indeed Hildesheimer's last cohesive text. *Nachlese* (1987) is merely a compilation of the notes that remained in his "Zettelkasten" at the end of his literary career. Baumgart describes the notes as herbs without the food in which they belong; they entice but do not satisfy (1987). Little attention has otherwise been paid to this slender paperback book, whose text is included in Volume 1 of the *Gesammelte Werke* (457-88).

The notes might entice a reader familiar with Hildesheimer's writing to identify where they might have been included. Some are aphoristic and as intriguing as the *Mitteilungen an Max*. Some are as confessional as revelations in *Tynset* or *Masante*. Jehle tells us that the idea for this compilation originated with an essay that

Hildesheimer contributed to the *text + kritik* volume of 1986 devoted to his work (in Arnold 1986, 8-18), and more than anything else the fragments confirm the writer's conclusive decision to stop writing literature (1990, 212). Be that as it may, the *Nachlese* will surely be able to tell us more about Hildesheimer's literary intentions as we examine what he excluded from his texts.

4: Dramas

THE FIRST AND MOST prominent subgenre of drama with which Hildesheimer's name is identified is the Hörspiel. He wrote more than twenty radio plays, most of them between 1952 and 1965, a time when radio had an important role in reconstructing cultural and literary life in postwar Germany. Movie houses, theaters, and concert halls left standing in 1945 lacked the equipment or properties for performances. Newspaper and publishing houses, when intact, lacked paper stock (Schwitzke 1963, 259). Radio broadcasting, the only form of public communication immediately available, was especially well organized in North Germany, which was under the control of the British. Daily news and lectures in higher education were transmitted, and eventually the Hörspiel was reintroduced. This form of drama had first appeared on German radio in 1923, the year the first radio station began broadcasting. It enjoyed a "Blütezeit" (height of popularity) from 1929 to 1936 before the "Anschluss" with Austria and the Nazi occupation of Europe (46-86).

The first postwar radio play, Wolfgang Borchert's *Draußen vor der Tür* (translated as *The Man Outside*) aired on North German Radio on 13 February 1947. Response to the broadcast was so favorable that radio plays became a regular monthly feature. South German Radio began to broadcast radio plays in 1948. By 1952 it was airing two plays per week, a circumstance that stimulated writing but encouraged facile, forgettable plots and characters (294). Many of those plays and their authors are no longer remembered and were certainly never considered for the Hörspielpreis der Kriegsblinden (Radio Play Prize of the Warblinded), a literary honor that originated in 1951. Hildesheimer received the 1955 prize for *Prinzessin Turandot*.

Hildesheimer adapted some of his radio plays, including *Prinzessin Turandot*, for the theater and for television production, but he also wrote original stage plays, the most famous of which, *Mary Stuart* (1970; published 1971), has been performed in English translation in the United States. Most critics regard this drama and all of Hildesheimer's plays after the mid1950s as examples of theater of the absurd. Hildesheimer enunciated his definition of the absurd in interviews and talks published in 1959, 1962, and 1967.

The absurd, according to Hildesheimer, is reality itself, which extends into the future and offers us no hope. The absurdist writes to show readers the illogicality of life as the constant that it is. The absurdist writes because writers of so-called realistic drama do not tell us that the world teaches us nothing. Hildesheimer himself writes from a deep conviction about the quality of life. In his plays he dramatizes the type of situation we can find in his short stories (1991a, 6, 826-28). This last is an important point, for it establishes Hildesheimer's view of himself as a writer of the absurd almost from the beginning of his career.

Jehle, who was Hildesheimer's archivist from 1982 to 1990, does not accept the self-assessment. The writer merely went along with early theatrical reviewers who labeled him an absurdist, he surmises, so that the political commentary in his plays would receive more attention (1990, 295). Jehle maintains that the stage versions of *Pastorale, Die Uhren* (The Clocks), and *Der schiefe Turm von Pisa* (The Leaning Tower of Pisa) have been misclassified as absurd, and that they are not at all imitative of Ionesco, Beckett, or even Grass. Instead, they reveal the development of Hildesheimer's characters from self-mockery to a mocking melancholy. During this period the writer was depressed. The plays express his extreme uncertainty about the value of his artistic work (275-76). Jehle's point of view contrasts markedly with all the criticism evaluated below.

In addition to his own dramatic work, Hildesheimer prepared adaptations for the stage. In 1961 he translated or adapted two plays by Richard Brinsley Sheridan (1751-1816), one by Carlo Goldoni (1707-1793), and one by William Congreve (1670-1729) for both radio and the stage.

A. Hörspiele

The earliest radio plays adapt themes or episodes from other sources. *Das Ende einer Welt,* a radio opera (1953), *Das Atelierfest* (1955), *Die Bartschedel-Idee* (1957), *Herrn Walsers Raben* (1960), and *Nachtstück* (translated as *Nightpiece,* 1964) are related to stories in *Lieblose Legenden. Das Ende kommt nie* (The End Will Never Come, 1952), *Begegnung im Balkanexpress* (1953), and *An den Ufern der Plotinitza* (1954) were inspired by situations that occur in *Paradies der falschen Vögel. Prinzessin Turandot* (1954) is loosely based on the Persian *A Thousand and One Nights; Das Opfer Helena* (1955) retells the story of the Trojan War; *Monolog* (1964) and *Es ist alles entdeckt* (All Has Been Discovered, 1965) are excerpts from *Tynset; Maxine* (1969) is based on *Masante; Mary auf dem Block* (Mary on the Scaffold, 1971), which was never published, is the radio version of the stage play, *Mary Stuart*.

Die Toten haben es gut (The Dead Have it Made, 1955) is an original work. Hildesheimer withdrew the play after its first broadcast, and it has never been published. *Pastorale, Die Uhren* (both 1958), *Der schiefe Turm von Pisa* (1959), *Unter der Erde* (Under Ground, 1962), *Hauskauf* (House Purchase, 1974), *Biosphärenklänge* (The Sound of the Spheres, 1977), and *Endfunk* (The Last Radio Broadcast, 1980), are the other original radio plays.

Jehle is the editor of a collected edition of most of the radio plays published in 1988. Not included are *Das Ende einer Welt, Es ist alles entdeckt, Endfunk, Pastorale, Die Uhren,* and *Nachtstück*. The "Nachwort" (afterword) to the collection is an abbreviated form of the text in the elaborately detailed drama chapter of *Werkgeschichte* (1990, 213-380), and this latter source is invaluable. For example, Jehle gives a synopsis of the unpublished *Es ist alles entdeckt,* as well as *Die Toten haben es gut* and *Die Herren der Welt* (The Rulers of the World), both of which have never been produced. He traces themes, images, characters, and key concepts from one radio play to another, to the prose works, and to Hildesheimer's personal life with assurance and a ready display of knowledge. This chapter, with its archival details, is the only comprehensive examination of Hildesheimer's radio plays.

Heinz Schwitzke's limited discussion of the plays through 1962 has some anecdotal value, but he was writing while the genre of the absurd was still developing and before substantive statements could be made about its effect. Schwitzke was head of the "Hörspielabteilung" (Radio Play Department) of North German Radio in Hamburg after 1951 and published an informative history, *Das Hörspiel,* in 1963. He asserts that, like many writers, Hildesheimer was stimulated by Ionesco. When *Pastorale, Die Uhren,* and *Der schiefe Turm von Pisa* first appeared in theaters in 1958 and 1959, critics apparently did not know about Hildesheimer's earlier prose texts or that these plays were originally written for radio. They described him as another Ionesco, but Schwitzke believes that the plays are satires, like the Hörspiele from which they were adapted. They reflect the same attitude as the stories of *Lieblose Legenden* and are influenced by Friedrich Dürrenmatt, the Swiss playwright, whose concept of the grotesque has nothing to do with Ionesco. It is verbal-intellectual, while the latter's grotesqueries are based on mimicry of the visible world. In Schwitzke's view, Hildesheimer is far more of a literary playwright than Dürrenmatt or Max Frisch; the static quality of his dialogues, as a result, makes adaptation for the stage difficult (1963, 385-90).

Hildesheimer's Hörspiele were the most popular of the German plays broadcast in translation to England (403). He, Max Gundermann, and Fred von Hoerschelmann brought international fame to German radio plays up to 1962 (129-30). It should come as no surprise that English audiences preferred Hildesheimer to, say, Eich, Frisch, or Dürrenmatt, for his writing is witty and understated, in contrast to the "typisch deutsche 'Tiefbohrerei' " (typically German sledgehammer style) of writers who were not educated abroad (403). The cosmopolitan quality of Hildesheimer's prose was noted as early as 1952 (see Morriën 1971, 85).

Schwitzke imparts valuable information about Hörspiel production and reception, but he bases his evaluation of Hildesheimer's writing style and what he considers its satirical intent on an awkward restatement of Ionesco's absurd point of view (in an essay he does not identify; see 377-78). His knowledge of Ionesco's work, in any event, is not extensive. He mentions only one radio play, *Le Salon de l'automobile* (see 385, 466). It is not at all clear whether Schwitzke really understands the genre of the absurd, especially since he refers so frequently to the grotesque (see the chapter "Das Groteske ist nicht das Absurde" in Heidsieck 1969, 37-46).

Puknus refers briefly to *Begegnung im Balkanexpress* and *An den Ufern der Plotinitza* as mocking satires whose theme is the sad state of political and historical affairs in the world (1978, 32), but these variations on the plot of *Paradies der falschen Vögel* receive little attention from critics. Hanenberg, for instance, does not mention these two plays. Jehle contributes the information that the protagonist of *An den Ufern der Plotinitza* is the last of Hildesheimer's artist figures able to influence political affairs. He describes the play as an attack against the press more virulent than a similar denunciation in Heinrich Böll's *Die verlorene Ehre der Katharina Blum* (translated as *The Lost Honor of Katherine Blum*, 1974) (1990, 247-49).

The general theme of the two 1954 *Turandot* plays for radio may be malicious mockery of the despotism of power, as Puknus reads the stage play (1978, 33), but Hanenberg can find the contemporary situation in Germany reflected in several specific themes: injustice, guilt, war, and misguided or inappropriate religious attitudes (1989, 40).

Pastorale, Die Uhren, and *Der schiefe Turm von Pisa*, which aired in 1958-1959, are better known in their stage versions and will be discussed in Section B below.

Das Opfer Helena, somewhat rewritten in 1961 and 1965 after its initial broadcast in 1955, is more consciously critical of social conditions than the Turandot plays, Puknus asserts, and Helena is a stronger figure than the false prince; but she, too, has no effective

influence on her society (1978, 39). Unable to avert the war by acting
authentically, Helena loses faith in humans and resigns herself to
the inauthenticity of the "they-world" in which she lives. Her
passivity at the end of the play resembles that of narrators in the
stories in *Lieblose Legenden* (Stanley 1983, 117).

Helena's story of the Trojan War illustrates how historians can
distort events, Hanenberg writes, and the author wants us to apply
this realization to the recent past. Helena and Turandot, involved
as they are with war and guilt, are Hildesheimer's skeptical contributions to "Vergangenheitsbewältigung," a literary theme in
which he had little faith (1989, 52-55; see also Dücker 1976, 27-28).
Jehle regards the play as the beginning of a conscious effort to grap-
ple with World War II. Hildesheimer identifies with Helena in an
attempt to see himself as a non-Jew who lived through the Hitler
years in Germany and can relativize the question of guilt (1990, 61-
62).

In *Herrn Walsers Raben* (1960) the writer introduces his first reflective narrator, Adrian Walser. This Hörspiel is a variation on
the theme of "Wie ich mich in eine Nachtigall verwandelt habe"
(translated as "Why I Changed into a Nightingale"), one of the
stories in *Lieblose Legenden*, and reveals Hildesheimer's solution
to the depression he had been experiencing. Adrian, who bears the
same name as the painter in *Landschaft mit Figuren* (Landscape
with Figures), does not free himself from the prevailing situation,
as the painter does. Instead, he gives in to a gentle melancholy
(1990, 303-4). After the late 1950s all of Hildesheimer's characters
abandon efforts to escape reality, for the writer's objective now is to
demonstrate their eventual downfall ("Untergang"). Certainly,
there are no more happy endings.

Hanenberg combines his evaluation of *Herrn Walsers Raben*
with what he said about the plays that preceded it, all of which relate to conditions after 1945 and express in grotesque and absurd
("sinnwidrig") terms the uselessness of knowing that the present is
corrupted by guilty people with false morals (1989, 73-75). He does
not contribute to the controversy about whether or not any of them
belong to the genre of the absurd.

Both Puknus and Jehle regard the husband and wife of *Unter
der Erde* (1962) and Helena as similarly disillusioned and resigned
to distrust and misunderstanding. Puknus reminds us that Hildesheimer seldom shows contented lovers. The husband and wife
momentarily acknowledge their love in the underground castle,
but when they discover an exit, they resume their bickering
(Puknus 1978, 54; Jehle 1990, 316). Or do they? The last several lines
of dialogue can also be read with a certain amount of tenderness
indicative of a future more serene as a result of the underground

experience. Hildesheimer has left to the discretion of the director whether the performers snap at each other or remain to some extent as solicitous as they were when they thought they were trapped underground. Linda M. Hill is the only critic to date who has read the ending in this manner; she notes without elaboration that there is a "happy end" (1976, 211, footnote 5).

Bernd Scheffer, whose essay, like Hill's, deals with stylistic matters, is noncommital. Marital controversy is one facet of the action, but because of the changes and displacements that make up the "Transpositionsvorgang" in Hildesheimer's writing, the meaning of the disagreements and of the play itself becomes problematical (1971, 19-22). *Transposition* is a term Hildesheimer uses in "Über das absurde Theater" (see 1984a, 16; 1991a, 7, 18). It equates with what Hill describes as "the association of ideas and images" (1976, 76). For Jehle the term means an inner logic of images (1990, 278-79).

A comparison of the deceptively monothematic bickering in *Unter der Erde* with the repartee of *An den Ufern der Plotinitza*, for one early example, would reveal a development to dialogue that is witty but capable of probing the emotional currents below the surface in a relationship. *Unter der Erde* bears comparison, too, with Beckett's *Play*, written in 1962-1963 (see Beckerman 1986, 152).

Monolog (1964), despite its title, has minor speaking parts for two women. The protagonist, Martin, is a reflective narrator; except for his name, he is similar to the anonymous narrator of *Tynset*. Indeed, the majority of his soliloquy appears again in that work, published a year later. As a result, this thematic variation has received little critical attention. Only Hanenberg and Jehle comment on it.

The past from which Martin is trying to extricate himself is of a more private nature than in prior works. What he has to say about Christian and Jewish religion is clear, harsh, and refers unequivocally to the Nazi past, which Hildesheimer confronts here for the first time. The speaker, like the narrator of *Vergebliche Aufzeichnungen*, seeks a place that has no history, and – like the narrator of *Tynset* – he retreats conclusively to his bed (see Hanenberg 1989, 109-12; Jehle 1990, 322-26).

The setting and characters of *Maxine*, first broadcast in 1969 but not published until 1988, come from *Masante*. This radio play is not simply an excerpt from the book, however. Several thematic strands – among them religion and the "Häscher" – do not appear in the radio play. More important, it does not have a necessarily negative ending. The narrator's conversation with a man who has returned from the desert leaves the impression that the narrator, too, may be able to find his way back to the inn.

Critics who discuss Maxine's role in *Masante* almost unanimously view her as related to the narrator. She is described as a projection (Neumann 1973, 497), an alter ego (Petuchowski 1975, 131), or a replacement for the narrator (Blamberger 1985, 85). Only Dücker and, surprisingly, Jehle see her as an independent and contrasting figure (Dücker 1976, 100) and even "großartig" (splendid; Jehle 1990, 111). When Jehle evaluates the radio play, however, he changes his mind about Maxine and reads the dialogue of the Hörspiel as a split monologue. Apparently he regards this radio play as an experimental prelude to the double monologue of *Hauskauf* (1974) (see 1988, 450-51; 1990, 331).

It may be that *Maxine* is experimental in a more general way that Jehle does not notice. The possibility of its positive conclusion supports Wetzel's suggestion that the *Masante* ending need not be negative (1979, 162). Add to these two possibilities the friendlier tone that might prevail at the end of *Unter der Erde*, and the glimmer of a positive trend emerges in Hildesheimer's writing that has not yet been explored in any detail. Dücker, Puknus, and Jehle sense it in various works, and Stanley specifically refers to the writer's "tentative absurd hope" (1994); but this facet of Hildesheimer's work deserves attention, particularly since he has a reputation for pessimism. The headline of a review of *Mitteilungen an Max über den Stand der Dinge und anderes*, for example, is "Ich bin ein grosser Pessimist" (Affentranger 1984).

Dücker notices a hint of optimism in *Hauskauf* (1974) when Speakers A and B refer to Williams, who functions as a wishful image of possible action (1976, 107). Puknus suggests in his 1978 book that A and B voice the opposing thoughts of a single mind (117), and he expands that insight in an article several years later (1986, 109-12). Andersson contributes a general comment: there is no peace or sense of personal well-being in this play because all plans to halt crimes against humanity would necessitate using the same means as the criminals and would thus be crimes (1979, 169).

Hildesheimer read the parts of both A and B when *Hauskauf* was broadcast by Bavarian Radio in 1974, supporting Jehle's declaration and the Puknus suggestion of 1978 that the dialogue is a two-voiced monologue. Speakers A and B do indeed share so many interests that they could be the same person. The differences between the narrator and Maxine, however, make it difficult to accept Jehle's idea that the same sort of double monologue occurs in the earlier radio play (1990, 353, 331).

By the end of *Hauskauf* both A and B want the house, which represents the world. In this way they show their melancholy acceptance of the approaching end of the world (Jehle 1990, 358). Hanenberg's interpretation is similar (1989, 174-78). Puknus prefers the term *resignation* to *melancholy*. He points out that A and B take compensatory pleasure in the house's well-stocked wine cellar and its kitchen outfitted with splendid copper utensils. When the wind ceases at the end of the play, it is an indication that the two speakers are content to have a house in which to take refuge for as long as possible. Speaker B's seemingly casual reference to Saturn in the night sky signals the inevitable destruction of the world (1986, 111-12).

Biosphärenklänge (1977) is a more radical expression of the lethargic attitude Puknus identifies in *Hauskauf*. In this play one becomes more aware of the innocence of the individual in society, who is forced to comply with circumstances caused by others and is punished along with these others for their acts. Hildesheimer may want to tell us that the innocent are actually guilty for doing nothing to oppose the technological spoilers of the earth, a modernization of the Hamlet situation that preoccupied him earlier in his career (Puknus 1978, 124-25). The husband and wife are so compatible that they will be able to understand each other without talking after they stuff their ears with cotton to block out the sound of the spheres. Their relationship is unusual for a Hildesheimer work and adds a positive image to the unrelenting negativity of the situation. Puknus wonders whether the writer, by giving his readers this positive image, is appealing to them to do something before the end (1986, 113-14). Hanenberg would say no. The impetus of this radio play is not hope that the end can be halted but an attempt to bring dignity to the certain end through our consciousness of it (1989, 181). Jehle, however, would probably say yes. The very fact that Hildesheimer wrote the play indicates that he felt the end could be averted (1990, 377). The hint of hope for a future noted here and elsewhere could be regarded as an aspect of Hildesheimer's worldview that draws him closer to Camus.

Except for the comments evaluated above and brief reviews by Petuchowski and Valentin Herzog in the collection of essays edited by Jehle (1989, 276-77, 280, respectively), there are no substantive interpretations of *Biosphärenklänge. Endfunk* (1980) has also received little attention. This play embodies the logical consequence of *Biosphärenklänge*, for there is no dialogue. A man sits before a radio. Its various stations fade in and out as technical difficulties interfere with the broadcast of weather and agricultural reports, religious messages, and musical programs (original music by Jan Wisse). The radio finally crackles into silence. Hanenberg and Jehle agree that when the play ends hope for a future ends, too. In *Endfunk* Hildesheimer shows us the future that he predicted in his first radio play, *Das Ende kommt nie* (Hanenberg 1989, 173). With his last play he shows us the consequences of our life-style as drastically as possible, for he does not want to have to reproach himself for not having warned us of the "Endzeit" (Jehle 1990, 380).

The radio plays have not attracted as much critical attention as the stage plays or the narratives, in spite of their initial popularity. Critics' disinterest is especially noticeable with regard to the thematically related *Hauskauf*, *Biosphärenklänge*, and *Endfunk*. Given the social commentary that Hanenberg finds, we have reason to read the radio plays more carefully, even from a deconstructionistic point of view, and to include them in our discussions of other genres. Consider, too, that when Hildesheimer indicates some hope for the future in these Hörspiele, he does it almost exclusively within a marital context. The contrast in the quality of personal relationships in the Hörspiele and in Hildesheimer's reflective fiction is worth investigating. The role of humor and understatement in the dramatic writing is another topic for contrastive study (see Dücker 1976, 96-97, for a brief excursus on the comic element in the stage plays).

Das Ende einer Welt (1953), a radio opera, is an adaptation of the short story of the same title. It was written in collaboration with Hans Werner Henze, who prepared a second version of the opera for a 1965 stage performance, changing the libretto to conform somewhat to the 1962 version of the story. Hildesheimer made corrections to Henze's libretto, but there is no way to establish the extent of his contribution to the revised opera, which is not published (Jehle 1990, 241).

B. Stage Plays

The first adaptation of *Prinzessin Turandot* for the stage, *Der Drachenthron*, (The Dragon Throne, 1955), presents the issues of hypocrisy in religion and the consequences of war more clearly than the Hörspiel versions, but the play's comic, even slapstick, features overshadowed its message in performance (see Gatter 1955; Hanenberg 1989, 42-43; Jehle 1990, 218). The power of language becomes power through language in this play, according to Andersson. Those in authority use language to transform what they tell the public into the public's reality (1979, 110-11).

The second adaptation, *Die Eroberung der Prinzessin Turandot* (The Conquest of Princess Turandot, 1961), is an unusually successful comedy with the happy ending that *Der Drachenthron* lacks. Although a utopian conclusion is unusual for Hildesheimer, it serves two purposes in this play; it highlights the charm and verbal brilliance of the dialogue, and it emphasizes the power of words.

We are left with the hope that the false prince and Turandot will have some influence on their world (Puknus 1978, 36). (See Lorenz 1986, 90-95, for a discussion of changes Hildesheimer made to the story as told by Gozzi, Schiller, and the librettists of Puccini's opera.)

The *Turandot* milieu mirrors the world of postwar Germany even more clearly than the radio play versions of the tale, Hanenberg writes. Entangled references to religion, power, guilt, action, reality, and the distant past culminate in love between the false prince and Turandot, who turns over rule of China to the real prince and Pnina. She and the false prince, a man of words and not deeds, will become their advisors. The play is a triumphant display of the power of reflection over action. Everyone is satisfied in the end. The apparent lack of motivation for such a joyful conclusion is intentional. We are to realize that reality is not like this. When the false prince tells Turandot that no chronicle will mention them in their role as advisors, he is right, for they do not exist (1989, 49).

Hanenberg's conclusion is reminiscent of the caption "Ceci n'est pas une pipe," which the surrealist René Magritte wrote beneath his painting of a pipe in the late 1920s. Hanenberg does not mention Magritte (or Foucault, who wrote an essay based on that painting and correspondence with the artist; see Foucault 1983) or further pursue his comment, but it could become the basis of a stimulating discussion of the ambiguity of language in this play and its contribution to the questioning of representation that distinguishes postmodernism.

Jehle, who combines radio, stage, and television versions of the Turandot material in his discourse, contrasts the comic features of the 1955 stage play with the social criticism and cultural satire of the 1961 and 1963 productions. In the last version he finds an insight that will be repeated by the narrator of *Tynset*; the false prince comments that the possibilities for action continually decrease (1990, 213-22). Jehle is always helpful in directing us to related texts.

Manfred Lauffs ignores the fact that Turandot freely surrenders her right to rule China. For him the happy ending has a melancholy tinge because the lovers do not become the rulers. His comment that the writer is so disillusioned with reality that he seeks refuge in myth is more responsive to the text (1986, 106-7; see also Hanenberg 1989, 39). Neither Lauffs nor Hanenberg compares Hildesheimer's treatment of this subject with Bertolt Brecht's *Turandot oder Der Kongreß der Weißwäscher* (Turandot or The Congress of Whitewashers; Esslin 1971, 102). It is noteworthy that both playwrights chose to adapt the same material at nearly the same time. A comparative reading could be enlightening.

The stage version of *Das Opfer Helena* premiered in 1959, in the midst of *Prinzessin Turandot* revisions and the appearance of the plays published as *Spiele, in denen es dunkel wird* (Plays in which Darkness Falls). Puknus admires the light, humorous tone of *Das Opfer Helena*, which reminds him of *Prinzessin Turandot*, but he also senses a reflective melancholy resignation in the title role and feels that theater critics undervalued this play and *Prinzessin Turandot* because of the emphasis placed on humor in performances (1978, 36-37). Ludwig Gatter, for example, complains about the provincialism of the real prince's imitation of Hitler in the 1955 production of *Prinzessin Turandot* (1955). It is not clear how much Hildesheimer participated in preparations for each production, but he was apparently influenced by Gatter. His stage directions for *Das Opfer Helena* include the notation that King Menelaos's bellicose attitude should not mimic Hitler (see Hanenberg 1989, 52). When *Das Opfer Helena* was to be staged in 1968 as a chamber musical (score by Gerhard Wimberger), he did not take part in adapting the script (Jehle 1990, 266).

Scholars, too, have apparently been influenced by reviews of performances. Although Christoph Lorenz mentions the "Absurdität und Fragwürdigkeit der Welt" (absurdity and questionable aspects of the world) that are unmasked in an unspecified version of *Prinzessin Turandot* (1986, 95), neither he nor other critics discuss elements of the absurd in any of its versions. Certainly, if one thinks of Ionesco's *The Chairs* or *Rhinoceros,* there is no visual comparison. There is reason, however, to regard the Turandot plays and both radio and stage versions of *Das Opfer Helena* as precursors of a discursive type of absurd that Martin Esslin describes in *The Theatre of the Absurd* (1969), although he does not connect it with Hildesheimer. Esslin names Jean-Paul Sartre and Albert Camus as the chief proponents of the type, and he contrasts it with an artistic or poetic version of the absurd that "tends ... toward a poetry that is to emerge from the concrete and objectified images of the stage itself" (7). Ionesco, Beckett, and Hildesheimer exemplify this type (see 6-8, 226).

Esslin's discussion of Hildesheimer is limited to the plays that were published in 1958 as *Spiele, in denen es dunkel wird: Landschaft mit Figuren, Die Uhren,* and *Pastorale oder die Zeit für Kakao* (Pastorale or Time for Cocoa, 224-26). While these plays are strikingly visual depictions of the "senselessness of life, of the inevitable devaluation of ideals, purity, and purpose" (6), it is misleading to assume that they are the only examples of the absurd in Hildesheimer's stage career or even the most typical examples. Dramatic works surrounding and following these plays reveal the same discursive, even philosophical, propensity that Esslin attributes to Camus. It would be well worth the effort to make a comparative study of the radio and stage versions of *Das Opfer Helena* and the Turandot radio, stage, and television scripts between 1955 and 1963, to determine how Hildesheimer's absurd orientation develops. After all, most critics acknowledge that it is fully realized in 1961 in *Die Verspätung* (translated as *The Delay)*.

Jehle, Hildesheimer's former archivist, argues that the writer is not an absurdist at all. At the time he wrote the plays of the *Spiele* group he was suffering from depression and just beginning to adapt his formerly repressed memories of the Nuremberg War Crimes Trials into what eventually became *Tynset*. Plays written around the same time show his despairing attempt to defend himself against the realization that we are not capable of directing our destiny in a world made up of bits and pieces of a system so dynamic that there is no longer any place ("Zwischenraum") where one can feel protected (1990, 275-302). *Zwischenraum* is a term from *Tynset*: "Nichts ist das, wo Zwischenraum ist und sonst nichts" (Hildesheimer 1965c, 181; 1991a, 2, 104). (See Hart-Nibbrig , for an unrelated examination of the aesthetics involved in *Zwischenraum.)*

It is Jehle's unique contribution to Hildesheimer research that he finds the writer in his writing, but in doing so he creates a paradoxical situation: he identifies a worldview that resembles the absurd as defined by Camus, and yet he insists that Hildesheimer is not a writer of the absurd. The controversy that has surrounded Hildesheimer's plays from premiere to the present is not resolved with Jehle's assertion, since he does not show that depression prevents a writer from adopting an absurd point of view. He offers no proof that would refute the contrary interpretations.

Two of the three plays published in *Spiele, in denen es dunkel wird* are united by the presence of a workman who replaces clear glass panes in each dwelling with dark glass. The other play, *Pastorale oder die Zeit für Kakao,* a reworking of *Die Herren der Welt,* takes place out of doors under a sky that darkens. *Die Herren der Welt,* which Hildesheimer discarded but did not destroy, was published for the first time in the *Gesammelte Werke* (1991a, 6, 73-167). Hanenberg is the only scholar who refers to the original text in his discussion of *Pastorale* (1989, 66-71).

The trio of plays established Hildesheimer's reputation with the public as an absurdist. Paradoxically, the plays are least characteristic of Hildesheimer's literary career – not because they are absurd but because Hildesheimer did not continue to pursue a visual, "poetic" depiction of the absurd. At the time he published *Spiele, in denen es dunkel wird* he was also working on the interplay of ideas that appears in *Das Opfer Helena* and *Die Verspätung.* The writer was, in fact, extremely preoccupied with his literary career in 1958 and 1959. In the latter year he completed or published or saw the production of one radio play, four stage plays, one play for television, the translation of a novel, two prose pieces, and six essays (see Jehle 1984, 11). If he felt uncertain about the value of his writing and suffered from depression, as Jehle claims (1990, 284, 288), he was also experiencing a burst of creativity that resembles the accomplishments of 1955 (see Jehle 1984, 9). We have, in fact, no objective data to corroborate Jehle's revelation of an artistic crisis. It is not noticeable in Hildesheimer's work. Jehle recognizes this lack of evidence, but he discounts it. He expresses surprise, in fact, that Eich, a close friend, did not notice the artistic break between the "depressiven" plays of 1958 and *Herrn Walsers Raben* of 1960, which, according to Jehle, shows that a reflective sort of melancholy mood is Hildesheimer's way out of his depression (1990, 303).

One could easily turn Jehle's comments around and declare that reflective melancholy in *Herrn Walsers Raben* and *Das Opfer Helena* and all plays after 1959 reveals depression, while the plays of *Spiele, in denen es dunkel wird* show active efforts to deal with reality. It is textually much easier to support this contention than to agree with Jehle, whose biographical interpolations are most intrusive in this section of *Werkgeschichte* as he attempts to eliminate the label of absurd from Hildesheimer's literary career. Whether or not Hildesheimer was emotionally distressed during the period of composition of the plays in the *Spiele* group, it does not follow that these plays cannot be regarded as belonging to the genre of the absurd. On the contrary, the absurd is a verbal and visual expression of its creator's awareness of distress (whatever its origin), transformed into an autonomous experience that will produce an experience in us. Whoever reads or watches one of Hildesheimer's plays looking for evidence of the playwright's depression invokes the intentional fallacy and seriously devalues the playwright's highly conscious use of language (see Hill 1976, 67-92). Other than Hill, no critic agrees with Jehle that Hildesheimer is not an absurdist.

Those who witnessed performances of the plays in the *Spiele* group were almost uniformly displeased with what they regarded as attempts to imitate Ionesco (Goldschmidt 1958; Luft 1959) or at the least to rework his themes (Ebert 1971, 94-95; Jacobi 1971, 96-98). The most useful information to come from newspaper reviews is that the plays are not theatrical. *Pastorale oder die Zeit für Kakao* is "anti-dramatisch" (Süskind 1958); *Landschaft mit Figuren* lacks dramatic tension (Luft 1959); its characters are abstractions and the performance is intellectual, not scenic (Karsch 1971, 101).

And yet it was these plays that made Hildesheimer famous. The talks he gave (and later published) to describe his concept of the absurd formalized the genre in Germany. The first of these talks, "Über das absurde Theater" (1984a,9-19; 1991a, 7, 13-26), was given at the University of Erlangen in 1960, where a student production of *Die Uhren* was part of a weeklong festival of plays. (See Chapter 5 for further discussion.)

Koebner, an early and frequently cited critic, notices a contradiction between Hildesheimer's theory and its execution. Theater of the absurd wants to show the viewer that the world has no answer to our questions, but the *Spiele* plays take a satirically superior attitude to socially accepted forms, and the plays are mockingly critical rather than objective (1971, 38-39). With this judgment Koebner sets the pattern for the controversy of social satire versus absurd that divides the critics, but even among those who read the plays as absurd there are differences of opinion.

Dücker, one of the few who does not refer to Koebner, points out that Esslin's conclusion – the plays are "far from free from rather obviously drawn analogies and somewhat facile conclusions" (1969, 226) – is itself facile, since it is based on so little evidence (1976, 4). Dücker makes two important points in his introductory section. First, the passivity of Hildesheimer's absurd protagonists is a hallmark of his perception of the absurd. Hildesheimer's writing is a parable about man's feeling of strangeness in the world, where the meaning of creation is hidden from us. Second, the absurd is the author's personal viewpoint, and his works are therefore autobiographical, but Hildesheimer is merely exemplary of the practical application of the absurd in life. It is not necessary to examine biographical data to understand what he writes (34-36).

Dücker's approach is sociological. He wants to determine what each work reveals about the social reality in which it exists. For example, *Pastorale*, in its 1965 version, tells us that attempts to alter society may lead to shifts of personnel within the system, but they do not change the structure of society (52-55). In *Landschaft mit Figuren* the deterioration of the persons sitting for their portrait represents a social system that is no longer vital. The light that slowly fades is a scenic expression of systemic decline to mere ideology (see 59-61). In *Die Uhren* the husband and wife try to overcome their alienation by imagining themselves as the people passing outside their window, but their lives do not change. The repetitive motive of rain indicates the unalterability of their existence, a theme central to all three plays (63).

Since each of the three plays has a distinguishable plot and character development, none of them is absurd, according to Hill, whose opinion – so markedly different from Dücker's – appeared also in 1976. Her crisp and compact definition is not well grounded (10-12), but her analysis of Hildesheimer's language is a major accomplishment. She effectively counters criticism about the nonsense or the lack of context in dialogues by identifying numerous eighteenth- and nineteenth-century quotations, the cultural context of the international clichés, and the stylistic devices that Hildesheimer utilizes as he "loosens the semantic connection among words while preserving the syntax" (75-76).

One distorting device that helps explain the associative quality of the dialogue is what Hill calls a "portmanteau phrase." An idiom included in a sentence shifts the grammatical function of a word common to the idiom and the obviously intended statement and creates a confusion of meaning. The characters, who "listen to each other well enough to catch at least one possible meaning" in what they hear, respond associatively. Someone will give a literal response to a rhetorical question, for example (80-85).

Hill's opinion is included in a book – *Language as Aggression: Studies in Postwar Drama* – in which she analyzes plays by several postwar dramatists, none of whose names appears on the title page. That may be why her work is not cited by other scholars. It is, however, valuable. She establishes a link between plays that seemed to be isolated experiments in the absurd and Hildesheimer's later prose. What she describes as "weathered quotations and slogans" of the eighteenth century or earlier (67-69) gives more – and early – evidence of the writerly play with intertextuality that distinguishes so many Hildesheimer works and that may be the most outstanding feature of his writing.

There is a biographical flaw in Hill's essay that is particularly noticeable in light of Lea's 1989 essay: Hill observes that Hildesheimer is better qualified to write documentary drama than other playwrights in Germany because his background as translator at the War Crimes Trials gives him more familiarity with "NS war criminals" (61). The remark is superficially accurate, but Hill betrays an insensitivity to Hildesheimer's Jewish heritage (if she knew of it) in supposing that – because he knew about the Holocaust from the persons who planned it – he could write about it. Lea performs a vitally needed service for Hildesheimer scholarship by outlining the ramifications of the writer's work as a translator at Nuremberg (1989, 51).

Andersson's theme is alienation within the absurd, but his references to the grotesque in Hildesheimer's dramatic technique are more interesting. The *Spiele* plays reveal an alienation effect whose intent is far from Brechtian, he writes. Where Bertolt Brecht wants to instill in the audience a desire to change obvious social problems, Hildesheimer means to unmask the obvious to show that it is based on unalterable inhumane assumptions. In *Pastorale oder die Zeit für Kakao*, for example, the characters, all business leaders, reveal how they have sacrificed their feelings for an ideal and been manipulated by a business world of such grotesque proportions that they must turn to the ideal world of art (music) for emotional release. And yet, because of the dominant role of the intellect, they dare not give way to unbridled feelings as they respond to music, for they risk losing control of the "Kampf ums Dasein" (struggle for existence) that determines their existence in capitalistic society (1979, 57-62; see also Weinhold 1983, 338-39).

References to *Landschaft mit Figuren* are scattered throughout Andersson's study, but his basic interpretation appears in Section 18 (129-36). This play makes a positive statement, but it does not have a happy ending; in fact, it has no ending at all. (Adrian's preparations to begin another painting constitute the same sort of *da capo* conclusion that Beckett later uses in *Play*, written between 1962 and 1963 [see Beckerman 1986, 152]. The persistent notion that Hildesheimer imitated other European absurdists can be refuted simply by checking the dates of their respective works.) Adrian, who has the courage to keep trying to capture the essence of "Dasein," is quite different from the married couple in *Die Uhren*. They retreat from a world whose hostility they accept even more conclusively than the artist of "Das Atelierfest" in *Lieblose Legenden*. Section 12 of the Andersson book (80-89) includes a noteworthy discussion of the couple as strangers in the world.

Andersson prefaces his comments with summations of the theoretical background of his arguments, including Arnold Heidsieck's *Das Groteske und das Absurde im modernen Drama* (1969). This work, as the title suggests, establishes the parameters of the two aesthetic categories, often regarded as indistinguishable, and rebuts Wolfgang Kayser's definition of the grotesque, which Heidsieck finds lacking in substance. Heidsieck, however, completely ignores Hildesheimer's plays in his discussion of both the grotesque and the absurd. For the latter he includes dramas by Beckett, Ionesco, and Fernando Arrabal translated into German and infers that there is no purely German version of the absurd in the late 1950s. His lack of knowledge of avant-garde German theater is inexplicable. Andersson relies on the Heidsieck argument, but Dücker (who notes Heidsieck's failure to mention Hildesheimer) prefers Kayser's definition of the grotesque in *Das Groteske: Seine Gestaltung in Malerei und Dichtung,* (The Grotesque: Its Formation in Painting and Poetry, 1957) because Heidsieck does not explain to his satisfaction why the absurd is a separate expressive category (1976, 129, footnote 21).

The distinction between what is grotesque and absurd in Hildesheimer's writing deserves more consideration. It was, for example, completely ignored by Hill, although *Pastorale oder Die Zeit für Kakao* is subtitled "Groteske in einem Akt." To further complicate the issue, she introduces the term *fantastic* in her concluding remarks (1976, 92). (See Heidsieck 1969, 30-33, for an explanation of the difference between "das Phantastische" and the grotesque.)

Andersson's conclusions sometimes resemble Dücker's, but he does not mention the latter's book, published three years earlier. It might not have been available when he wrote his work, given the time lag that can occur between submission of a manuscript for publication and its appearance on the market.

Perhaps Ulrike Weinhold did not have access to Andersson's book when she prepared the essay that was published in 1983, but the Dücker and Hill interpretations were certainly available. As she outlines her understanding of the absurd, she quotes from sources cited also by Dücker, Hill, and Andersson (among them Adorno, Heidsieck, Taëni, Ehrig, and Koebner), but she does not mention her predecessor scholars. Her essay is marred by failure to examine these thoughtful interpretations.

Weinhold's thesis is that of the plays in the *Spiele* collection, *Pastorale oder die Zeit für Kakao* and *Landschaft mit Figuren* are not works of the absurd but social criticism, and *Die Uhren* is a not yet completely successful attempt at the absurd as exemplified by Beckett and Ionesco (1983, 342). Weinhold uses the song in *Pastorale oder die Zeit für Kakao* to display her point of view. Labeled "ein idiotisches Quartett" in an early review by Wiegenstein (see Andersson 1979, 62), it contains bits and pieces of quotations from various sources and clichés that Hill identifies in her tour de force of cultural detective work. Weinhold considers the song nonsensical, a clear indication of the emptiness of the speakers and what they have to say. The three plays do not depict the absurd dialectic of meaning and meaninglessness that is evident in Beckett's *Waiting for Godot*, where dialogue hovers between the banal and the significant. Instead, they are mere montages of senseless dialogue and clichés (338-39).

Of the two most recent critics, Hanenberg has very little to say about the early plays beyond noting that the world of *Landschaft mit Figuren* is recognizable as the recent past and the guilt-laden present (1989, 63). Jehle reports that Hildesheimer exploits his hallmark associative flow of images for the first time in *Pastorale oder die Zeit für Kakao,* and he surmises that the technique is based on Djuna Barnes's prose style in *Nightwood,* published originally in 1937 (Hildesheimer's translation, *Nachtgewächs,* was published in 1959). An inner logic and not the plot determines the arrangement of images in the play, but Jehle does not expand on this subject and is apparently unaware of Hill's text. The minimal role of graphic art in *Pastorale oder die Zeit für Kakao* signals the author's pessimism, which comes to the fore in these three plays and remains evident for the rest of his literary career (1990, 278-80).

In Jehle's reading of the ending of *Landschaft mit Figuren* the author only pretends to lighten the mood by lifting the darkness; actually, by having Adrian refuse to give up painting, he may be indicating his regret that he became a writer. The one-act play *Die Uhren* represents the nadir of Hildesheimer's depressive period. This play is marked by the sense of horror one feels when one cannot find a way out of a situation (1990, 285-88).

Die Uhren and another one-act play, *Der schiefe Turm von Pisa* (originally, like *Die Uhren* and *Pastorale oder die Zeit für Kakao*, a Hörspiel), premiered together in 1959. Reviewers of the double bill might have asked themselves if the latter play was added solely to give the audience something "lustig" (cheerful) after the weak and unimpressive example of absurd theatrics in *Die Uhren* (see Baer 1959; Jacobi 1971, 96-98). The more lively play has been ignored since then, in spite of its favorable reviews. Until recently it was available only in the journal *Akzente* (1959), although the plays surrounding this one began to appear in book form prior to performance. It is radically different from the plays of the same period, and only Jehle and Hanenberg devote any attention to it.

Jehle tells us that *Der schiefe Turm von Pisa* was the first play Hildesheimer wrote after he resolved the crisis of his depressive period and decided to return to graphic art, since literary art cannot effect change. Jehle offers no evidence from the play itself, however, to support his contention that Hildesheimer believed that literary art is useless. He was, after all, writing, and in this instance he wrote an amusing play with a seemingly satisfactory ending, as the authorities imprison all the negative characters. For Jehle the happy ending is merely a form of self-deceptive therapy (1990, 288-93).

Hanenberg wants us to recognize that the supposedly positive figures – those who take pleasure in art – display a far from admirable "Schadenfreude" at the end of the play. There is no indication of a utopia, and in fact the police inspector's ruthless handling of the guilty parties should provoke fear in the audience (1989, 72-73). Readers who wish to make their own judgment about the merits of this short play will find it in the *Gesammelte Werke* (1991a, 7, 275-306).

According to clippings in the archive and reviews in Rodewald (1971), critics at the premiere of *Die Verspätung* in 1961 applauded the play as successful theater of the absurd. Except for Koebner and

Jehle, readers of the play agree. There is considerable difference of opinion, however, about why this play is successful.

Die Verspätung may seem to be absurd in the first of its two parts, Koebner writes, but then it becomes markedly melancholy as Hildesheimer modifies his technique of using paradox to unsettle his audience. The professor, tormented by the fact that everything has already been invented or is well known, expects a triumph with the "Guricht." When it reveals itself as a harmless bird and the professor dies, the play moves out of the sphere of the absurd. It becomes a psychological and existential drama. The hero wants to conquer his alienation, to fit in with the rest of the world. In his vanity he is a comical figure, but when he confesses his alienation he gains dignity (1971, 39-42).

Dücker reads the play much as Koebner does, but he maintains that it projects an absurd world both visually (as the villagers perceive it) and existentially so far as the intellectual – the professor – is concerned. The "Vertreter" (sales agent), who wants to integrate the professor into society, behaves hypocritically, reveals that he is Möllendorf, and only confirms the intellectual in his belief that society is absurd. Dücker's reading is not convincing, and his reference to "Psychologie des Intellektuellen" at the conclusion of his interpretation suggests that the play may indeed be more of a psychological study than a work of the absurd (1976, 63-69).

Andersson's contribution is unusually valuable, for he unabashedly addresses the issue of imitation raised by the theater critic Henning Rischbieter, who wrote after the premiere of Die Verspätung that it was a clever but late copy "ganz à la Ionesco" (quite in the manner of Ionesco; 1961, 12). Although Rischbieter found resemblances to Hildesheimer's short story "Der Urlaub," he maintained that the play was epigonous (see Andersson 1979, 99-100; 189). Andersson answers the charge by connecting the play not only to the Lieblose Legenden story (which was first published separately in 1951), but to the Spiele, in denen es dunkel wird, and to the talk, "Über das absurde Theater," as he proves that the play is true to Hildesheimer's particular view of life as incomprehensible (1979, 89-102).

Weinhold refers to Beckett more often than to Ionesco, as she explains that Hildesheimer finally achieves the absurd in Die Verspätung because his protagonist is not historically identifiable. He failed with Pastorale oder die Zeit für Kakao, Landschaft mit Figuren, and Die Uhren, which are examples of satire, because the boundaries of reality were not exceeded (a point that Hill also makes; see 1976, 89).

Beckett's Vladimir and Estragon in *Waiting for Godot* are not simply outsiders, they are beyond social categorization. The professor, like them, becomes a "Nicht-Held," a no-one in the sense of historical and social determinations. Like them, he is a traveler who has fallen out of time and space orientation. His negativity vis-à-vis life contains the positive value of his disavowal of all appearance. This is the first time that Hildesheimer has created a positive position that can be held up as a measure of judgment of illogical life. Such a position cannot then offer sensible alternatives. The professor's effort to oppose his construct "Guricht" to the figurativeness of life places the uselessness of a search for meaning alongside the nothingness of the apparent meaning of existence (1983, 353-58). It is Weinhold's position that Hildesheimer did not realize for a long time that there is no historical or social dimension to the absurd.

According to Christoph Lorenz, who brings several new insights to this discussion, *Die Verspätung* can be characterized as a dramatic fantasy about the isolation of modern individuals. Although the sets are traditional, the play converts slowly to an absurd event, says Lorenz in an interpretation that is diametrically opposed to Koebner's. The village inhabitants play roles that resemble a "Volksstück" (folk play) as they approximate the banality of daily life. Hildesheimer then reveals the greed, corruption, and lust beneath their empty clichés. At the end of the play only the casket maker remains as a living symbol of the unavoidable power of death and birth (1986, 97-98).

Lorenz is one of the few critics who takes an interest in the casket maker (Andersson is another; see 1979, 98-99). He turns to the Gnostics to explain this character's function. A manual laborer, like the glazier in two plays of the *Spiele* collection, he is the demiurge responsible for the incompleteness of the world. A figure between the absolute goodness of God and evil, it is he who created an error-ridden world where glass falls out of windows, as it does in *Landschaft mit Figuren*. Hildesheimer uses a demiurge figure to depict the doubtfulness of the world, which he wants us to ponder. In a way Hildesheimer himself is the same demiurge, for he steps between the doubtful world and humanity to demonstrate that humanity is a stranger in the cosmos (101). Lorenz offers additional impetus for the study of religion in Hildesheimer's collected works with his reference to Gnosticism.

It is the contemporary relevance of *Die Verspätung* that interests Hanenberg, who is unaware of Weinhold's theory of the absurd as ahistorical. He agrees with Koebner that the play is a turning point in Hildesheimer's career, but for the reason that this play enunciates what earlier works only intimated: that it is useless to strive because wars instigated by power figures determine our reality. The village of Dohlenmoos has diminished in size with each of several wars, and its inhabitants flee from yet another war at the beginning of the play. Their lives are organized around the precarious, horrible, nonsensical acts that take place even as nations talk about peace (1989, 84-86).

The "Guricht" of *Die Verspätung* equates with God and Godot, as Jehle reads the play, but it is a utopian vision that comes to nothing. The professor's impatient wait for the "Guricht" is merely waiting for the inevitable downfall ("Untergang"), and thus the negative principle survives in this play, not the positive (1990, 310-13). Jehle does not mention Weinhold, who finds positive value in the play.

The genre issue remains a point of contention in interpretations of *Nachtstück* (1964), whose protagonist is related to the speaker in *Monolog*, the radio play that aired in 1964, and the monologist of *Tynset* (1965). It is thus not surprising that Koebner describes the play's protagonist as Godlike, wearing his isolation as if it were a halo and holding the power to end his life with his store of medicines (1971, 47). Goll-Bickmann's discussion of the *Tynset* narrator's godlike role-playing may be applied to the stage and radio plays, as well (1989, 262-90; see also Andersson 1979, 107).

Dücker notes that the sleepless man of *Nachtstück* is much like Professor Scholz-Babelhaus of *Die Verspätung* in his isolation and frustration. The intruder, like the "Vertreter" a socializing agent, tries to convince the protagonist of the value of the world's "Ersatzantworten" (substitute answers), using his cultural background to mask the substitute quality of the answers he gives (1976, 73-74). Puknus, among others, agrees that the intruder is the embodiment of the world from which the sleepless man has retreated and the victor in the end. The sleepless man is spared the professor's disillusionment, but only because he had already renounced any fixed idea and had fled reality (1978, 74-76; see also Andersson 1979, 106; Lorenz 1986, 99; Jehle 1990, 320-21).

The sleepless man pays a high price for being without sin; isolated from his fellow human beings, he suffers a loneliness that brings him nightmares when he does sleep. He cannot return – like Adrian in "Der Urlaub" – to a society where everyone else believes the "Ersatzantworten" of organized religion. If to be free of sin is meritorious, it is also devastating, for the man is unendurably lonely (Andersson 1979, 102-3).

Weinhold reads *Nachtstück* as a fully developed work of the absurd. The criticism of contemporary European society in this play is so clear, however, that it is almost as if Weinhold did not really read the play. References to the red-robed Church leaders, for one example, have a relevance at least as obvious as, if not more obvious than, any of the images in the *Spiele* collection of plays, because the role of the Catholic church during World War II was a current topic. Rolf Hochhuth dramatized the Church's silence in *Der Stellvertreter* (translated as *The Deputy*), a documentary drama that premiered in 1963, just a year before *Nachtstück*. Surely there could be no question in the mind of any viewer or reader at that time about the connection between the sleepless man's vision of the cardinals and the Church's silence as the Jewish population of Europe was exterminated.

Hanenberg calls attention to two textual elements that prove *Nachtstück's* specific ties to the recent German past. First, when the protagonist thinks of the larger-than-life authority figures from the executive, legislative, and judicial systems who were his ideal of manliness, he remembers that these figures overthrew democracy and instituted fascism. Confused and with a sense of loss he rejects his former ideal. Second, when he focuses on memories, he has a reason to escape through medication. When he does not think about the past, there is no external history, but still he cannot sleep. Historical events drive him to attempt to escape, but he cannot, because those who make history are right there in his room, represented by the figure of the intruder. If the intruder were not there, the play would be absurd. As it is, the play deals with concrete events suffered in the past and their continuation in the present (1989, 103-7).

Whether or not Hanenberg would agree with Weinhold that the absurd is ahistorical, he persuasively rebuts her claim that *Nachtstück* is ahistorical by offering examples of current events reflected in the play. To support his opinion that Hildesheimer entered a more pointedly expressive phase vis-à-vis fascism in the 1960s, he quotes from Hildesheimer's 1964 review of *Der Stellvertreter*. Hochhuth's play, an example of documentary theater popular in the 1960s (see Hill 1976, 90), dramatizes the role of the Catholic church in World War II as a Jesuit priest tries in vain to persuade Pope Pius XII to protest the deportation of the Jews in Rome. The priest, who accompanies a group that is shipped to Auschwitz, is executed before a sympathetic SS officer can free him. Hildesheimer bases his negative review on the play's realistic representation of a real event. It is not that the play is badly written, he argues, but that it presents the material improperly. The loathsome nature of the plot would have to be transposed (by means of "Verfremdung") into an even more intense horror to be taken seriously on the stage. In its present form the play makes the events farcical (Hildesheimer 1991a, 7, 298-302).

Hanenberg points out that it is not so much Hochhuth's play that interests or upsets Hildesheimer but the relationship between the Church and fascism that Hochhuth depicts in specific detail (1989, 96-99). Hildesheimer takes the opportunity presented by the review to discuss the significance of this relationship in his own way, and he dramatizes it in his own way in *Nachtstück*.

A theater critic's remark that he thought he was watching a Beckett play until halfway through *Nachtstück* (Karasek 1971, 111) adds credence, on the one hand, to Weinhold's assessment of the two plays as successful theater of the absurd. On the other hand, the historical relevance that Hanenberg finds in these plays – which contradicts Weinhold's theory of the absurd – and the various pro and contra readings described above, including Jehle's unilateral judgment that Hildesheimer is not an absurdist, point to the need for a far more detailed look at the absurd as Hildesheimer defines and portrays it. His plays have a recognizable social and historical significance that individualizes his vision of the absurd but surely does not invalidate it. *Mary Stuart*, the only specifically historical play, is even more problematical than *Nachtstück*, for it is based on Hildesheimer's premise that history itself is absurd.

The essay "Anmerkungen zu einer historischen Szene" (Notes Regarding a Historical Scene), which appeared in the program for the premiere of *Mary Stuart: Eine historische Szene* in Düsseldorf (1970), and in translation in Los Angeles (1973) and New York (1981), was no doubt meant to enhance a viewer's appreciation of the play, for its simultaneous dialogue makes heavy demands on an audience. Dücker wonders whether Hildesheimer was uncertain about the effect the play would have and prepared the essay to clarify his views on historical writing (1976, 88). According to Hans Schwab-Felisch, what Hildesheimer does in the play is to refute his own claim that, because we cannot know what they were thinking, history teaches us nothing about persons from the distant past. On the contrary, he creates a Mary Stuart who is a significant and imaginable queen (1971, 133-34). Somewhat similarly, Dieter Gerber hears ambiguous irony in the subtitle of the play and in Hildesheimer's claim that the action he presents must have happened, no matter how improbable it might be (1970). For Ulrich Schreiber the play is an unsuccessful attack on the myths and documents that surround Mary, Queen of Scots. Hildesheimer aestheticizes her death and does not surpass Schiller. Schreiber has high praise for the return to ensemble acting in this play (1971, 137), which confirms the report of a reviewer of the Schweinfurt performance in 1973 that Swinarski, who was also the director in Düsseldorf in 1970, did not play the scenes in simultaneous dialogue, as written (M. K., 1973).

In the Rodewald interview of 1971 Hildesheimer said that he realized that the "Anmerkungen" had little to do with the play (Rodewald 1971, 150). Many theater critics, such as Schwab-Felisch, had already come to the same conclusion (see Puknus 1978, 110), but not all later critical readers agree with them or even with Hildesheimer. While several scholars simply bypass the play-wright's commentary when they discuss this complex drama, Dücker uses the essay to establish what is and is not absurd about its dialogue and action. *Mary Stuart* is not theater of the absurd, in his opinion, but it does have absurd characteristics. One of them is its simultaneous dialogue, which shows the equal value of what-ever happens on stage. Hildesheimer uses the servants to make the absurd understandable, and he has Mary take a tranquilizing drug for the same reason. Mary herself cannot logically be accepted as absurd, however, for she is only an object to be used by a subject. In the end, the determination of whether or not this work is theater of the absurd depends solely on the historical, social, or philo-sophical standpoint of the determiner (1976, 90-92). In this regard Dücker follows Norbert Oellers, who declares that those who con-sider life and history as absurd will find the play absurd (1971, 77).

Puknus's 1978 book is useful as a source for opinions published earlier than 1977, but Puknus does not take a stand on many issues, including whether or not *Mary Stuart* is a work of the absurd and the applicability of the "Anmerkungen" to the play. He detects a secret "erhöhendes Pathos" (elevating pathos) in all characters, in-cluding Mary, but he is not sure what to make of it. Unfortunately, he does not explain what it is that constitutes the pathos that he detects in all of Hildesheimer's writing after the mid1950s (145).

Stanley is obviously one of those who believe that life and his-tory are absurd. For her there is no question about the genre to which *Mary Stuart* belongs. Esslin's term "madness of the times" – as exemplified here by simultaneous dialogue, exaggerated self-interest, and frenetic activity – describes the sixteenth-century absurd world of the play and establishes its thesis. The antithesis is Mary's triumphantly soaring prayer just before her execution, "for the reader experiences a warmly human sudden and unexpected empathy," but no synthesis of emotions occurs (Stanley 1979b, 113-14; Esslin 1969, 363).

We do not experience Mary as a person because Hildesheimer employs a "Verfremdungseffekt" to keep us at an objective distance from the queen and the play. Still, there are two moments when audience identification does occur: one of them is the prayer; the other is just prior to the prayer, when Didier re-covers the *chaise percée* so that no one in the execution audience will discover that the queen is incontinent. At least, Stanley hopes that he acts out of respect for his queen, "because he seems the only genuine character on stage" (1979b, 111).

Helene Scher does not identify with Mary but instead emphasizes her "role playing" as gracious queen, true believer, and finally martyr. The "Anmerkungen" are a useful guide to the events in the play, but Scher suspects that the author included the notes mainly to avoid being criticized for his historical inaccuracies (1980, 173-74). She mentions a wrong date and misquotations and their function in the absurd situations that develop onstage, but she does not regard the play as absurd (165) and concludes that Hildesheimer "expresses his own version of the dialectics of history" in the play, which she compares technically with Ferdinand Bruckner's *Elisabeth von England* (1930) (170).

According to Weinhold, *Mary Stuart* is a "Psycho- und Historiogramm" that has no claim to the designation of absurd (1983, 361).

In Hanenberg's reading of the play, Hildesheimer attempts a historical reconstruction that challenges us not to believe history and therefore not to learn anything from it. *Mary Stuart* parallels *Tynset* as it shows us that neither fiction nor documentation can make history imaginable, although to make it imaginable one would have to have both of these elements (1989, 143-44). Since he is not interested in whether or not the play is absurd, Hanenberg would not contradict Weinhold, but Axel Schalk unintentionally does. He devotes a chapter to this play within a 1989 study of several contemporary German plays based on historical fact. Schalk not only accepts the absurd as the philosophical framework for the play but stresses the play's ties to Camus's definition of the absurd (128). As he describes Hildesheimer's demythologizing of the queen, Schalk also points out the writer's implicit criticism of Schiller's idealistic vision of her in the drama that premiered in 1800 in Weimar. Hildesheimer clothes Mary as Schiller did but shatters the Schillerian illusion of beauty by having a rat jump out of her skirts (131; see also Scher 1980, 166; Jauß 1982, 797-806).

Both Hanenberg and Schalk focus on the demythologizing aspect of the play (see also Greif 1973, 76-88). This facet of Hildesheimer's writing plan gains more prominence in the Mozart biography of 1977 and *Marbot* in 1981 (see Faber 1980; Arens 1986; Stanley 1988). Schalk, however, introduces a new consideration when he joins Hildesheimer's dramatic writing to the tradition of cynicism that prevailed around 1830 among the writers of what was later labeled "Junges Deutschland" and "Vormärz." Schalk names Georg Büchner (1813-1837) and Christian Dietrich Grabbe (1801-1836) as the forerunners of Hildesheimer's dramatic intent (137); his comments here might well be used to counteract or at least to modify the complaints of Arens and others about Hildesheimer's failure to address social concerns in *Mozart*.

Mary Stuart marks the beginning of Hildesheimer's (auto)biographical phase, Jehle writes. The author does not identify with Mary but with her demeanor in the face of death, for by this time Hildesheimer had a positive response to death. Jehle refers to a television conversation with Walter Jens in 1968 in which the writer commented on the euphoria that runs parallel to anxiety when one contemplates death. Beginning with *Tynset*, death is a prominent figure in all Hildesheimer works (1990, 336-39).

There is a puzzling inconsistency in Jehle's explanation of the pharmacist's presence in the play. He writes that Hildesheimer considered accounts of Mary's composure so improbable that he introduced the fiction of a pharmacist, who would furnish tranquilizing potions (1990, 341). Mary, however, shows no fear before she begins to take the tranquilizers; she takes them without demur, but one might well ask whether she really needs them. We are invited to regard her actions at the end of the play as the result of the drugs she took, but they might have been unnecessary.

As a textual (absurd) device, of course, the pharmacist with his vials and liquids is one more manifestation of the exaggerated self-interest of the servants, who intend that the queen should die without pathos, as a sort of living résumé of their dedication to the cosmetic aspect of aristocratic life (see Stanley 1979b,110). Jehle's biographical background to the play might not include all of the playwright's motivation.

Mary Stuart is Hildesheimer's most sophisticated and most widelyproduced play, and the only one that has a historical background. The queen appeared earlier in his oeuvre in the short story "Schläferung" as one of the three women whom the narrator would choose to watch over him as he sleeps in his guitar (Hildesheimer 1991a, 1, 140-53). She is also the subject of a poem written in 1974 (1991a, 7, 554). She and Mozart are the only historical persons around whom Hildesheimer weaves a text to illustrate his thesis that, no matter what historians write, we cannot know anything about anyone who lived in the distant past. An investigation of the elements the two texts have in common would likely reveal more clearly than the "Anmerkungen" why Hildesheimer, as a deconstructionist, constructs his specifically historical texts without reference to social and historical issues (see Arens 1986, 167).

Dücker includes a short excursus on the comic in Hildesheimer's dramatic writing in his *Mary Stuart* chapter. He mentions instances in *Die Verspätung* and *Nachtstück* that, like exchanges between Mary's servants, produce comic relief (1976, 96-97). Hill observes that the dialogue in *Pastorale oder die Zeit für Kakao* sometimes approximates the studied irrelevance in Oscar Wilde's *The Importance of Being Earnest* (1895) (1976, 91). Gert Westphal, who directed Hildesheimer's first radio play in Hamburg, declares that Hildesheimer writes genuine comedy, and that his characters have a flair for the comic even when it is directed against themselves (1989, 169). This otherwise unexplored facet of Hildesheimer's dramatic voice deserves more emphasis.

Hildesheimer has been underestimated as a dramatist, probably because of the discursive quality of his dialogues, the opinion of at least one critic that drama is not Hildesheimer's "most characteristic medium" (Lea 1979, 19), and certainly because his early plays were erroneously regarded as imitative. The interpretations evaluated above could form the basis of a detailed study of Hildesheimer as a modernist who questions representation in language and whose elegant wit in the early plays might be "an intuitive perception of the absurd" (Ionesco 1964, 25) that develops into a unique formulation necessarily tied to history.

C. Television Plays

Three unpublished versions of stage plays were performed on German television: *Turandot* (October 1963), *Die Verspätung* (September 1969), and *Mary Stuart* (September and November 1974). The only television play that appears in Hildesheimer's collected works is *Karolin bei Nacht* (Karolin at Night), which was broadcast in Germany in September 1959, with the title *Nocturno im Grand Hotel*, and published with that title in 1959 and 1960. It has been completely ignored by critics, perhaps because the collections in which it was originally published are out of print. Jehle offers a brief summary of the amusing adventures of the ne'er-do-well, Karolin, an aspiring second-story man (1990, 267-69). Anyone interested in the scope of Hildesheimer's penchant for clichés has the opportunity to examine their proliferation in this play, now that it is available again (Hildesheimer 1991a, 6, 307-52).

D. Adaptations

Hildesheimer adapted two plays by Sheridan (*The School for Scandal* and *The Rivals*), and one each by Congreve (*The Way of the World*), and Goldoni (*Un curioso accidente*) in the period 1960 to 1982. All were published, but none is included in the collected works. The critical commentary for this aspect of Hildesheimer's career is contained in newspaper reviews, an article by Petuchowski on *Die Lästerschule* (*The School for Scandal*) (1987), Hildesheimer's notes to the two Sheridan adaptations (1991a, 7, 293-94, 295-97), and the pertinent section in Jehle's *Werkgeschichte* (1990, 424-60).

Petuchowski briefly describes the implications of scene changes, notes possible literary allusions in the name changes made, and concludes that the playwright's stylistic and scenic adaptations are important "because they reveal literary habits of the adaptor" (1987, 263). Jehle combines bibliographical thoroughness, biographical details, and critical insight in a section that is most certainly the starting point for any future research. One might, for example, develop Jehle's supposition that Hildesheimer wanted to corroborate – with his work on the English and Italian plays – the point he began to emphasize in *Die Verspätung*, that the problems of the future are the result of errors in the past that the present refuses to acknowledge (1990, 459).

Jehle says elsewhere (1990, 380) that Hildesheimer is at pains to warn us of the approaching end of life as we know it, which announces itself with a monotonous, piercing "G" in *Biosphären-klänge*. The writer did not completely give up hope of arousing the public after *Endfunk*. The most unusual of his adaptations was broadcast on television for what was, in all likelihood, the largest audience he ever had. His text, "Herr, gib ihnen die ewige Ruhe nicht " (Lord, do not give them eternal rest), is a revision of the Latin text of the sections of the *Requiem* (KV 626) known to have been set by Mozart. Hildesheimer read his version of the text following a performance of each section by the Orchestra and Choir of Swiss Television in a production of November 1986 seen in Germany and Switzerland. This textual adaptation is an uncompromisingly direct expression of the writer's belief that humanity is destroying the world (see 1991a, 7, 723-35).

A close reading of all of Hildesheimer's adaptations with his didactic goal in mind and with the aim of connecting the adaptations to the dramatist's earlier modernistic questioning of representation would establish more clearly than Jehle's excellent summary just how relevant these works are within Hildesheimer's oeuvre and in the history of drama itself.

5: Essays

THE SEVENTH VOLUME OF the *Gesammelte Werke* (1991) is labeled "Vermischte Schriften" (Miscellaneous Writings). It contains speeches on literature and music, poetry, book and play reviews, art-exhibit commentaries, travel descriptions, reminiscences, and what the editors identify as "Opinion Papers" ("Stellungnahmen") dealing with the environment. Most of the speeches have appeared elsewhere, for example in *Das Ende der Fiktionen* (1984), which is subtitled "Reden aus fünfundzwanzig Jahren" (Speeches of the Last Twenty-five Years). Volume 3 of the *Gesammelte Werke*, which is labeled "Essayistische Prosa," contains only the Mozart biography and related material ("Paralipomena und Materialien") consisting of previously published talks and essays on Mozart. The editors do not regard the short pieces in Volume 7 or the similar "Paralipomena und Materialien" in Volumes 4 ("Biographische Prosa") and 6 ("Theaterstücke") (Plays) as essayistic, but in fact all of this nonfictional material is stylistically similar to the prose of *Mozart*, which is personal and conversational and attempts to draw the reader into a shared reflective mood. Montaigne coined the word *essai* for his personal prose; the term is appropriated here to categorize the commentaries described above and gathered in Volumes 3, 4, 6, and 7 of the *Gesammelte Werke*.

Among these texts are commissioned reviews for journals, newspapers, and art catalogs. They qualify for the designation *essai* because Hildesheimer often used these opportunities as a springboard for opinions he wanted to publicize, a characteristic that Hanenberg mentions in connection with the review of Hochhuth's *Der Stellvertreter* (Hanenberg 1989, 96-100; Jehle 1990, 499). The art reviews, almost all of which are concerned with contemporary sculpture, painting, and even photography, were not in wide circulation before 1991. Jehle's chapter, "Hildesheimer und die bildende Kunst" (Hildesheimer and Graphic Art) in *Werkgeschichte* is the only source to date for information on the genesis and biographical background of these essayistic commentaries (see 1990, 492-510). Since all the artists Hildesheimer discusses, with the exception of Maurice Sendak, are relatively unknown in the United States, and one cannot easily compare Hildesheimer's comments with the works of art themselves, their scholarly appeal in America is probably limited to what they reveal about Hildesheimer's didactic intent in his nonfictional writing (see Jehle 1990, 477). The more significant essayistic writings relate to literature and humanity's destruction of the environment.

When *Das Ende der Fiktionen* was published in 1984, it was reviewed favorably in the press. Jehle includes two of these reviews in the collection he edited in 1989. Tilman Jens's general remarks resemble those in most of the newspaper and magazine articles on file in the archive (1989, 336-38). Baumgart's remarks, however, could be the foundation for a thorough analysis of the essayistic writing, particularly those pieces whose theme is the phenomenon of the absurd. Baumgart finds that, with the exception of "Über das absurde Theater," Hildesheimer's essayistic voice is tentative. His formulation of the absurd, on the other hand, is clearly thought out and decisive (1989, 339). The last statement is noteworthy for the reasons that follow.

Most critics who read Hildesheimer's prose as literature of the absurd (Haas, Dücker, Blamberger, and Andersson, for example) mention this essay and the others listed below to support their interpretations, and nearly every critic of the *Spiele* plays refers to "Über das absurde Theater"; the several essays on the absurd have never been evaluated as a theoretical corpus, however. In fact, the texts have never been printed together. Considering that they are the only such examinations of the genre in German, there is surprisingly little commentary surrounding them. The texts are:

"Empirische Betrachtungen zu meinem Theater" (1959) (Empirical Observations Regarding My Theater; 6, 820-23)

"Über das absurde Theater" (1960) (1984a, 9-26; 1991a, 7, 13-26)

"Die Realität selbst ist absurd" (1962) (Reality Itself Is Absurd; 1991a, 6, 826-28)

Frankfurter Poetik-Vorlesungen (1967) (Readings on Poetics, Frankfurt) which includes: "Die Wirklichkeit des Absurden," "Die Wirklichkeit der Reaktionäre," and "Das absurde Ich"[1] (The Reality of the Absurd, The Reality of the Reactionary, The Absurd I) (1991a, 7, 43-99).

Baumgart's comment about the decisiveness of Hildesheimer's writing in "Über das absurde Theater" casts doubt on the Jehle comment that Hildesheimer did not fully understand the absurd and wrote the essay only to identify himself with European theater

---

[1] Stanley's translation of the last essay ("The Absurd 'I'") appears in *Denver Quarterly* 15.3 (1980): 92-105.

of the absurd and thereby gain a wider audience for his political pronouncements. Jehle argues that the writer contradicts himself when he describes theater of the absurd as a representation of the absurd world and then states that each play shows only a portion of world events. Either each play is a full representation of the world, Jehle writes, or Hildesheimer's definition of the absurd play as a parable of world events is not valid (1990, 296-97; see also Weinhold 1983, 354).

The argument is shallow. It founders when one reads the entire essay, for Hildesheimer modifies ("Ich modifiziere also") what Jehle objects to. Each absurd play portrays the absence of sense in world events, and "das absurde Theater als Ganzes" that is, as a phenomenon, reveals the didactic intent of the parable of absurd theater, to which all absurd plays contribute (1984a, 13; 1991a, 7, 16). In other words, to appreciate theater of the absurd, the audience should be aware that an individual play belongs to the genre of theater of the absurd. Otherwise, a viewer will regard the play as absurd (that is, illogical) and not as a work of the absurd (1984a, 10; 1991a, 7, 14).

Jehle develops his own line of thought rather than the content of "Über das absurde Theater." He reads the essay as an expression of Hildesheimer's frustrated realization that he cannot enlighten others about social and political problems through the theater. At the time, beginning in the late 1950s, the writer was attempting to adapt his formerly repressed memories of the Nuremberg War Crimes Trials for literature and was extremely depressed. Jehle does not try to explain why Hildesheimer continued to describe himself as an absurdist into the late 1960s and even extended the scope of his talks (in the *Frankfurter Poetik-Vorlesungen* of 1967). When Hildesheimer protests, in "Die Realität selbst ist absurd," that he was never influenced by Ionesco (see 1991a, 6, 826-28), he is most likely trying to extricate himself from any alignment with the European absurdists and focus attention on his own definition of the absurd.

Jehle states unilaterally that the absurd phase of Hildesheimer's career is actually his depressive phase, in response to the recognition of an "Umbruchsituation" (reformulation situation) in his life, which presumably means that the writer had realized that his life was not proceeding as he expected (1990, 295-300).

Jehle and Weinhold are the most articulate of the critics who assert that Hildesheimer's writing does not belong to the genre of the absurd. It would be enlightening to compare and contrast their interpretations with those of Dücker, Blamberger, Neumann, and others who regard Hildesheimer as an absurdist, particularly since neither Jehle nor Weinhold refers to other scholarship on this issue. Baumgart's comment about the decisiveness of the essayist's voice in "Über das absurde Theater" provides a base from which to launch such an investigation.

Hildesheimer's theoretical essays on the absurd and his critical writing on the arts in general, as well as a number of very short personal notations and commentaries in Volume 7 not mentioned above, comprise an enticingly open area for research.

Hildesheimer's views on environmental issues have appeared in newspaper and magazine interviews and articles (see Jehle 1989, 36-38). His predictions of an "Endzeit" and his efforts on behalf of Greenpeace and other organizations probably made him more famous in the 1980s than he was in the late 1950s, when his absurd plays were introduced. Most of the essays of Volume 7 that deal with the environment are labeled "Stellungnahmen," but two very short pieces included under "Glossen" also deal with "Endzeit" predictions: "Greenpeace" (639-40) and "Ein tanzender Pessimist" (A Dancing Pessimist, 638). The editors place the adaptation of Mozart's *Requiem* text, "Herr, gib ihnen die ewige Ruhe nicht," among the "Stellungnahmen" (723-35), but it might have been better to include the adaptation in Volume 3 with the other Mozart material. It is significant, after all, that Hildesheimer chose a Mozart composition to bring his "Endzeit" message to the largest possible audience.

A slender book that appeared posthumously in December 1991 contains the speech Hildesheimer gave when he accepted the Weilheim Prize for Literature in the Spring of 1991. This prize is awarded by a jury of students at the Weilheim Gymnasium and is intended as a recommendation of the recipient's writing to other gymnasium students. Hildesheimer added a postscript for the students' parents when he prepared the talk for publication. He completed it shortly before his death, and it is tempting to speculate that he realized that it might be his last statement because its tone is different from other "Endzeit" predictions. He enunciates in the postscript his bleak view of the future, which he did not express in his speech before the young people, but he includes unusually esoteric references that give the postscript an impersonal aura. Hildesheimer distanced himself – this time – from his extremely personal theme by invoking his polymathic literary persona.

In *Werkgeschichte* Jehle refers to the writer's concern for the environment as it is reflected in various narrative texts, but he does not include the essays listed above in his otherwise comprehensive text. No one has made a study of Hildesheimer as an environmentalist, and yet it is as significant an aspect of the writer's career as his absurd stance.

All of Hildesheimer's "Endzeit" texts deserve consideration as a separate body of work. Included along with the essays listed above would be the radio plays *Hauskauf; Biosphärenklänge;* and *Endfunk;* the book *Mitteilungen an Max über den Stand der Dinge und anderes;* and the adaptation "Herr, gib ihnen die ewige Ruhe nicht." It could be fruitful – and it would be consonant with the references already made to Hildesheimer as a postmodernist – to study the implications of the "Endzeit" predictions as a variation of Zarathustra's admonition that we take better care of ourselves in "Von der Nächstenliebe" (Regarding Neighborly Love) of Nietzsche's *Also sprach Zarathustra* (1968, 73).

6: Translations

A. Narrative Fiction

THE SCOPE OF HILDESHEIMER'S prose translations reveals the catholicity of his reading. His English translation of a poem by Stefan George, published sometime between 1943 and 1945, was followed in 1946 by a translation of Franz Kafka's short story "Elf Söhne" ("Eleven Sons"). Next, he translated into German Frederick Spencer Chapman's *The Jungle Is Neutral* (*Aktion "Dschungel." Bericht aus Malaya*), which was published in 1952. Anne Piper's novel *Early to Bed* appeared in his German translation (*Jack und Jenny*) in 1955 and was reprinted several times (see *Works Consulted*). In 1959 he published a translation of the Djuna Barnes novel *Nightwood* (*Nachtgewächs*). In the 1960s he translated a book by Ronald Searle, five books by the cartoonist Edward Gorey, and a portion of James Joyce's *Finnegans Wake*. He published his translation of Samuel Beckett's "As the Story was Told" ("Wie die Geschichte erzählt wurde") in the early 1970s. Jehle provides this information in his chapter, "Hildesheimers Übersetzungen und Bearbeitungen" (Hildesheimer's Translations and Adaptations; 1990, 381-424, 484-92).

Hildesheimer discussed his role as translator in an essay that accompanies the Joyce translation ("Übersetzung und Interpretation einer Passage aus 'Finnegans Wake' von James Joyce" [Translation and Interpretation of a Passage from *Finnegan's Wake*]) and in the talk, "Der Autor als Übersetzer – Der übersetzte Autor" (The Author as Translator – The Translated Author) (1991a, 7, 338-51 and 211-17). Aside from Jehle's chapter and Hildesheimer's own comments, there is a paucity of critical attention to this aspect of the writer's career, which surely influenced his creative work. Two instances come to mind. One is the reference in *Tynset* to a cup "mit einer Träne Wein" in it (1965c, 24; 1991a, 2, 18), which is a detail borrowed from *Nightwood* ("The tear of wine is still in his cup ..."; Barnes 1961, 84). In his 'Nachwort" (afterword) to the translation Hildesheimer describes what impelled him to translate the novel (1991a, 7, 355-58). His incorporation of an image from the book in his own writing several years later reveals even more clearly how much he valued Barnes's writing.

The other example is the narrator's casual reference to Queen Mary's hat in *Zeiten in Cornwall*, which may be a tribute to James

Joyce and the reality he brings to *Ulysses* with the "trifling detail" of Leopold Bloom's hat (see "The Jewishness of Mr. Bloom," a talk given originally in English; 1984a, 197; 1991a, 7, 183). The hat appears again in *Masante* as one of Maxine's possessions, and this time it serves a double purpose. We can add to the associations surrounding the hat not only its apparent function as part of a descriptive passage in *Zeiten in Cornwall* but also the fact that a fictional narrator now refers to an object mentioned by a nonfictional narrator. The function of this blurring of distinction between fiction and nonfiction – and it occurs many times in Hildesheimer's writing – has yet to be discussed, but it certainly enriches a text and may, at least to some extent, be traced to the writer's translating interests. (For the *Zeiten in Cornwall* reference, see 1991a, 1, 377; for the *Masante* reference, see 1973, 202; 1991a, 2, 267.)

Hildesheimer as translator is a theme completely open to interpretation. It has, in addition, a timely appeal. When one of the Edward Gorey translations, *Eine Harfe ohne Saiten oder Wie man Romane schreibt* (A Harp Without Strings or How One Writes Novels, 1963), was recently reprinted, it garnered an elaborate review by Manfred Seiler in *Die Zeit* (18 October 1991) because the dry wit of Gorey's cartoons and the translated commentary have postmodern appeal. One possible topic for future research could be what the choices Hildesheimer made for his translating projects might say about postwar society and the writer's perception of his creative role during the 1960s, when several translated texts surround the first appearances of his reflective narrator onstage and in prose fiction. It would be worthwhile, too, to compare the themes of the translated works with Hildesheimer's own works of the same period and consider what the former contributed to the latter.

B. Plays

Jehle's *Werkgeschichte* is the only source of information on Hildesheimer's dramatic translations (1990, 424-60). According to the former archivist, Hildesheimer translated when he was at turning points in his literary career (425). Soon after the publication of *Tynset*, for example, he translated George Bernard Shaw's *Saint Joan* (*Die heilige Johanna*), which was published in 1965 and performed in 1966. In 1969, when he was also involved in shortening *Masante* and preparing *Zeiten in Cornwall*, he translated Shaw's *Arms and the Man* (*Helden*); he saw his work published and performed in 1970.

Unlike Peter Handke, who chose a contemporary writer (the American Walker Percy) for his translating projects (Zorach 1992, 69), Hildesheimer preferred to immerse himself in texts of the eighteenth and nineteenth centuries (or in any event, pre-World War II writing). He wanted to direct attention in this way to a past in which a better future seemed possible but in which the mistakes were committed that contribute to our own uncertain future (Jehle 1990, 427).

The translated plays are not, unfortunately, included in Hildesheimer's collected works, but they appear in new editions from time to time. In addition to telling us about the background to the writer's undertakings, Jehle alludes to parallels that one can find between the Shaw plays and Hildesheimer's own works (448-49, 452). That information as well as the author's "Anmerkungen des Übersetzers" (Translator's Notes) appended to the 1976 edition of *Helden*, might be the starting point for an investigation of the effect of the earlier writer on the later (Hildesheimer 1991a, 7, 406-7).

Conclusion

WOLFGANG HILDESHEIMER GAVE FAR more interviews – to newspaper and television journalists, critics, and students – than bibliographies record. He was unusually accessible and invariably gracious. I speak from personal experience, for I interviewed him in 1974 and have spoken with German university students who had the same opportunity in the 1980s. In all his interviews Hildesheimer openly admitted that his experiences played a part in the depiction of his fictional world; but his candor has not been entirely beneficial, particularly to the major works, *Tynset* and *Masante*. The writer's openness has resulted in a closed attitude that is just one of the many paradoxes in Hildesheimer's literary career, but it is crucial for understanding what he imparts to us.

Until recently critics forced the reflective prose into a confessional category where its sociocultural, historical, theoretical, even philosophical aspects were ignored. They brushed aside the works with an identifiable story (*Paradies der falschen Vögel* and most of the tales in *Lieblose Legenden*) as witty, sophisticated, but somehow inappropriate social satire for the post-1945 German reconstruction era. Reich-Ranicki's preference for literature engaged in confronting the German past more explicitly than Hildesheimer cared to do was shared by other critics, among them Durzak, who regretted that the writer had no constructive comments to make (1976, 310-11).

I do not mean to imply that speech-act theories are less than adequate interpretive tools. I notice rather that commentaries that concentrate on Hildesheimer as the narrator do so to the invariable detriment of the text. The language of the "I" in Hildesheimer's fictional and quasi-fictional writing is a metalanguage, but it does not, or not only, create the metatext that Jehle, for instance, reads as he constructs the writer's life from his writing.

Hildesheimer said many times that he could only write from the first-person perspective, but he did not say that he was thereby writing about himself. In fact, he might have been following Percy Lubbock's admonition, "Fiction must look true" (1969, 132), by situating it in an "I," the most potent indicator of the reality of the discourse presented. And that is exactly the point. We are to accept the discourse as reality-based – phenomenologically the situations presented are, indeed, real (Hamburger 1953, 329-33). There is a difference, however, between the reality of a narrative "I" and that of its author, who is separated from the narrator by what Félix Martinez-Bonati regards as an "abyss" (1981, 85). Cohn, who refers to both theorists in "Signposts of Fictionality: A Narratological Perspective," suggests that it would be eminently worthwhile to compare and contrast the Hamburger and Martinez-Bonati theories of fictionality (1990, 795-96). I suggest that Hildesheimer's narrative voice from *Lieblose Legenden* to *Masante*, with special attention to the *Tynset-Masante* complex, would be an ideal framework for such a discussion.

In the wake of early biographical interpretations of those works, Haas (1975), Hill (1976), Weisstein (1983), Schiff (1983), Beck (1986), and Hart-Nibbrig(1987) have inspected facets of the richly interwoven prose that Hildesheimer produces throughout his oeuvre, including its musical or collagelike structure. Dücker (1976), Andersson (1979), Blamberger (1985), Neumann (1986), and Stanley (1988) have explained why they read the prose as literature of the absurd. I have made suggestions throughout the present work for new research, particularly of a comparative nature. There is still much to be learned from Hildesheimer's writing, for example, the role of organized religion in his worldview and the power or powerlessness of language to express one's apprehension of the world and one's position in it, including our relationship to and responsibility for the natural environment.

Jehle writes that it was Hildesheimer's goal for a long time to warn us about the approaching "Endzeit," to show us as drastically as possible that we are destroying nature with our present life-style (1990, 380). The writer demonstrated his commitment to this goal after 1983 by adhering to an opinionated, essayistic writing style, which has its most dramatic impact in the blunt language of the 1986 televised talk "Herr, gib ihnen die ewige Ruhe nicht."

It is noteworthy that Hildesheimer reverted to the somewhat pedantic biographer persona of *Mozart* and *Marbot* when he included a Latin quotation from Cato in the postscript to the Weilheim speech for publication shortly before his death and thereby depersonalized his last "Endzeit" prediction (1991b, 28). By thus foregrounding his polymathic intelligence in his final personal statement about the environment, he directs our attention again to the allusions and interweavings that produce the hallmark intertextuality and "Überblendungen" of his writing. I suggest, finally, that this aspect of Hildesheimer's writing be investigated more thoroughly and with more specificity in the early stories, the novel, the plays, and the reflective texts. Some fine interpretive work has already been produced by narratologists, stylisticians, structuralists, and poststructuralists, but Hildesheimer's position in postwar European literary history has not been fully established because initial misunderstandings about his writing have obscured his goals. He began his career at a time when German readers were too close to their own experiences of World War II to be able to relate to his cosmopolitan first-person perspective and his avant-garde artistic writing style. At the end of his career, in spite of the success of *Mozart*, he was not as well known as he should have been (Michaelis 1991).

Hildesheimer's use of musical and collage methods, as well as his polymathic penchant for weaving other texts into his own, are as avant-garde now as they were in 1958, when he gained fame as a dramatist of the absurd. His idiosyncratic techniques and the insights they offer have not yet been fully examined. With the emphasis on language that distinguishes postmodernism, the literary critic since the 1970s can apply many new theoretical and philosophical concepts to texts. Some of these have already succeeded in revealing the open-ended indefiniteness of Hildesheimer's urbane discourse. As we continue to explore the writer's effort to communicate with us, these new insights into reading and writing will surely establish Hildesheimer's place in European and world literature.

Works Consulted

1. Works by Wolfgang Hildesheimer

1951, ed. *Trials of War Criminals before the Nuremberg Military Tribunals under Control Council Law No. 10. Nuremberg, October 1946-April 1949*. Washington: United States Government Printing Office 1951, 3: "The Justice Case" and 4: "The Einsatzgruppen Case"/"The RuSHA Case."

1952a. Chapman, F. Spencer. *Aktion "Dschungel." Bericht aus Malaya. Aus dem Englischen übersetzt von Wolfgang Hildesheimer*. Frankfurt am Main: Verlag der Frankfurter Hefte.

1952b. *Lieblose Legenden*. Stuttgart: DVA.

1953. *Paradies der falschen Vögel*. Munich: Desch (1967).

1955. *Der Drachenthron*. Munich: Desch.

1956. "Aufzeichnungen über Mozart."*Merkur* 10: 1033-53.

1958. *Spiele, in denen es dunkel wird*. Comprises *Landschaft mit Figuren, Pastorale oder Die Zeit für Kakao, Die Uhren*. Pfüllingen: Neske.

1959. Barnes, Djuna. *Nachtgewächs: Roman. Ins Deutsch übertragen von Wolfgang Hildesheimer*. Pfüllingen: Neske.

1961a. *Die Verspätung: Ein Stück in zwei Teilen*. Frankfurt am Main: Suhrkamp.

1961b. Piper, Anne. *Jack und Jenny*. Reinbek: Rowohlt.

1962a. Gorey, Edward. *Ein sicherer Beweis: Übertragung des Textes ins Deutsche von Wolfgang Hildesheimer*. Zurich: Diogenes (1981).

1962b. *Lieblose Legenden*. Frankfurt am Main: Suhrkamp.

1962c. Searle, Ronald. *Quo vadis? Textredaktion von Wolfgang Hildesheimer*. Munich: Desch.

1962d. Sheridan, Richard Brinsley. *Die Lästerschule: Lustspiel in zehn Bildern. Frei bearbeitet von Wolfgang Hildesheimer.* Munich: Desch.

1963a. Barnes, Djuna. *Nachtgewächs: Roman. Aus dem Englischen übertragen von Wolfgang Hildesheimer. Mit einer Einleitung von T.S. Eliot.* Frankfurt am Main: Fischer.

1963b. Gorey, Edward. *Die Draisine von Untermattenwaag: Übertragung des Textes ins Deutsche von Wolfgang Hildesheimer.* Zurich: Diogenes (1981).

1963c. Gorey, Edward. *Eine Harfe ohne Saiten oder Wie man einen Roman schreibt: Übertragung des Textes ins Deutsche von Wolfgang Hildesheimer.* Zurich: Diogenes (1981, 1990).

1963d.*Vergebliche Aufzeichnungen. Nachtstück.* Frankfurt am Main: Suhrkamp.

1964a. Gorey, Edward. *Das Geheimnis der Ottomane: Ein pornographisches Werk. Deutsch von Wolfgang Hildesheimer.* Zurich: Diogenes (1981).

1964b. *Herrn Walsers Raben. Unter der Erde: Zwei Hörspiele.* Frankfurt am Main: Suhrkamp.

1964c. Piper, Anne. *Jack und Jenny: Roman.* Berlin: Deutsche Buch-Gemeinschaft.

1965a. *Das Opfer Helena. Monolog: Zwei Hörspiele.* Frankfurt am Main: Suhrkamp.

1965b. Shaw, George Bernard. *Die heilige Johanna: Dramatische Chronik in sechs Szenen und einem Epilog. Deutsch von Wolfgang Hildesheimer.* Frankfurt am Main: Suhrkamp (1971, 1975).

1965c. *Tynset.* Frankfurt am Main: Suhrkamp (1973).

1966. *Wer war Mozart? Becketts "Spiel." Über das absurde Theater.* Frankfurt am Main: Suhrkamp.

1967a. Gorey, Edward. *Das unglückselige Kind: Ins Deutsche übertragen von Wolfgang Hildesheimer.* Zurich: Diogenes (1981).

1967b. Hildesheimer, Wolfgang. "Nightpiece." Trans. Wolfgang Hildesheimer. In *Postwar German Theatre: An Anthology of Plays,* ed. M. and G. Wellwarth. New York: Dutton, 277-313.

1968. *Begegnung im Balkanexpress. An den Ufern der Plotinitza: Zwei Hörspiele. Mit einem autobiographischen Nachwort.* Stuttgart: Reclam.

1969a. Gorey, Edward. *La Chauve-Souris Dorée: Deutsch von Wolfgang Hildesheimer.* Zurich: Diogenes (1981).

1969b. *Interpretationen: James Joyce. Georg Büchner. Zwei Frankfurter Vorlesungen.* Frankfurt am Main: Suhrkamp.

1970. Shaw, George Bernard. *Helden: Deutsch von Wolfgang Hildesheimer.* Frankfurt am Main: Suhrkamp (1977, 1985).

1971a. Barnes, Djuna. *Nachtgewächs: Roman. Deutsch von Wolfgang Hildesheimer.* Frankfurt am Main: Suhrkamp.

1971b. *Mary Stuart: Eine historische Szene.* Frankfurt am Main: Suhrkamp.

1971c. *Zeiten in Cornwall.* Frankfurt am Main: Suhrkamp.

1973. *Masante.* Frankfurt am Main: Suhrkamp (1975).

1974. *Hauskauf: Hörspiel.* Frankfurt am Main: Suhrkamp.

1975a. *Hörspiele.* Frankfurt am Main: Suhrkamp.

1975b. *Mozart Briefe: Ausgewählt, eingeleitet und kommentiert von Wolfgang Hildesheimer.* Frankfurt am Main: Suhrkamp.

1975c. *Paradies der falschen Vögel.* Frankfurt am Main: Suhrkamp.

1975d. *Theaterstücke. Über das absurde Theater.* Frankfurt am Main: Suhrkamp.

1976. Piper, Anne. *Jack und Jenny: Übersetzung von Wolfgang Hildesheimer*. Frankfurt am Main: Krüger [1955 without reference to translator].

1977a. *Biosphärenklänge: Hörspiel*. Frankfurt am Main: Suhrkamp.

1977b. *Mozart*. Frankfurt am Main: Suhrkamp (1980).

1978. "Mein Judentum." In *Mein Judentum*, ed. Hans Jürgen Schultz. Stuttgart: Kreuz.

1979a. *Exerzitien mit Papst Johannes.Vergebliche Aufzeichnungen*. Frankfurt am Main: Suhrkamp.

1979b. *Was Waschbären alles machen: Bilder von Rebecca Berlinger mit einer Geschichte von Wolfgang Hildesheimer*. Frankfurt am Main: Insel.

1980a. "Die Wahrheit der Unwahrheit." *Die Zeit*, 29 February, Feuilleton 17-18.

1980b. Piper, Anne. *Jack und Jenny: Aus dem Englischen von Wolfgang Hildesheimer*. Frankfurt am Main: Fischer.

1981a. Interview, *Der schweizerische Beobachter*, 15 June.

1981b. *Marbot*. Frankfurt am Main: Suhrkamp (1984).

1982. *Lieblose Legenden*. Frankfurt am Main: Suhrkamp (all twenty-six stories).

1983. *Mitteilungen an Max über den Stand der Dinge und anderes*. Frankfurt am Main: Suhrkamp.

1984a. *Das Ende der Fiktionen: Reden aus fünfundzwanzig Jahren*. Frankfurt am Main: Suhrkamp.

1984b. *Der Drachenthron: Komödie in drei Akten*. Zurich: Haffmans.

1984c. *Gedichte und Collagen*, ed. Volker Jehle. Bamberg: Fränkische Bibliophilengesellschaft.

1984d. *The Jewishness of Mr. Bloom. Das jüdische an Mr. Bloom. Englisch/Deutsch*. Frankfurt am Main: Suhrkamp.

1985. *Der ferne Bach: Eine Rede.* Frankfurt am Main: Insel.

1986a. Congreve, William. *Der Lauf der Welt: Deutsch von Wolfgang Hildesheimer.* Frankfurt am Main: Insel.

1986b. *Endlich Allein: Collagen.* Frankfurt am Main: Insel.

1987a. *In Erwartung der Nacht: Collagen.* Frankfurt am Main: Insel.

1987b. *Nachlese.* Frankfurt am Main: Suhrkamp.

1988. *Die Hörspiele,* ed. Volker Jehle. Frankfurt am Main: Suhrkamp.

1989. *Die Theaterstücke,* ed. Volker Jehle. Frankfurt am Main: Suhrkamp.

1990. *Mit dem Bausch dem Bogen,* ed. Volker Jehle. Warmbronn: Keicher.

1991a. *Gesammelte Werke in sieben Bänden,* ed. Christiaan Lucas Hart Nibbrig and Volker Jehle. Frankfurt am Main: Suhrkamp.

1991b. *Rede an die Jugend: Mit einem Postscriptum für die Eltern.* Frankfurt am Main: Suhrkamp.

1992. *Landschaft mit Phoenix: Collagen.* Frankfurt am Main: Insel.

2. Works Cited in Chronological Order

Baltrusch, Peter. 1955. "Turandot 1955." *Deutsche Zeitung* (Stuttgart), 27 April.

Gatter, Ludwig. 1955. "Prinzessin Turandot ist zu gescheit geworden." *Kölnische Rundschau,* 26 April.

Goldschmidt, Rudolf. 1958. "Zeit für Kakao: Hildesheimer-Uraufführung an den Münchener Kammerspielen." *Stuttgarter Zeitung,* 21 November.

Süskind, W. E. 1958. "Warten auf Hildesheimer." *Süddeutsche Zeitung,* 20 November.

Baer, Volker.1959. "Herrlich, dieser Turm." *Hannoversche Allgemeine Zeitung*, 20 April.

Emig, Erik. 1959. "Das Opfer Helena: Hildesheimer Uraufführung in Mainz." *Frankfurter Allgemeine Zeitung*, 15 July.

Luft, Friedrich. 1959. "Nur Ionesco kann so etwas." *Die Welt*, 2 October.

Barnes, Djuna. 1961. *Nightwood*. New York: New Directions Books [1937].

Hölderlin, Friedrich. 1961. *Gedichte. Hyperion*. Munich: Goldmann Verlag.

Rischbieter, Henning. 1961. "Hoffnung für das deutsche Drama." *Theater heute* 2.12: 12-14.

Courts, Gerd. 1963. " 'Nachtstück' von Wolfgang Hildesheimer." *Deutsche Rundschau* 81: 53-54.

Leisegang, Herbert. 1963. "Alpträume, die den Schlaf verscheuchen." *Generalanzeiger der Stadt Wuppertal*, 2 March.

Nöhbauer, Hans F. 1963. "Am Nullpunkt der Literatur." *Die Abendzeitung* (Munich), 6 August.

Schwitzke, Heinz. 1963. *Das Hörspiel: Dramaturgie und Geschichte*. Cologne: Kiepenheuer & Witsch.

Vielhaber, Gerd. 1963. "Gefängnis des Schlaflosen. Hildesheimers 'Nachtstück' in Düsseldorf uraufgeführt." *Kölner Stadt-Anzeiger*, 2 March.

Ionesco, Eugene. 1964. *Notes and Counternotes*, trans. Donald Watson. London: Calder.

Altick, Richard D. 1965. *Lives and Letters*. New York: Knopf, i-xiii.

Blöcker, Günter. 1965. "Stegreifspiel der Motive." *Merkur* 19: 486-87.

Domin, Hilde. 1965. "Denk ich an Deutschland in der Nacht." *Neue Deutsche Hefte*, 10 September, 124-34.

Kähler, Hermann. 1965. "Hildesheimers Flucht nach Tynset." *Sinn und Form* 17: 792-97.

Schulz, Uwe. 1965. " 'Tynset' oder Der Abschied vom Humor." *Frankfurter Rundschau*, 26 January.

Schwab-Felisch, Hans. 1965. "Wolfgang Hildesheimer/Tynset." *Die neue Rundschau* 76: 194-98.

Mann, Thomas. 1967. *Der Erwählte*. Frankfurt am Main: Fischer [1951], 281-474.

Nietzsche, Friedrich. 1968. *Also sprach Zarathustra: Ein Buch für Alle und Keinen*. Part 6, Vol. 1 of *Nietzsche Werke. Kritische Gesamtausgabe*, ed. Giorgio Colli and Mazzino Montinari. Berlin: de Gruyter.

Esslin, Martin. 1969.*The Theatre of the Absurd*. Garden City, N.Y.: Doubleday [1961].

Heidsieck, Arnold. 1969. *Das Groteske und das Absurde im modernen Drama*. Stuttgart: Kohlhammer.

Lubbock, Percy. 1969. *The Craft of Fiction*. New York: Viking Press [1922].

Schnurre, Wolfdietrich. 1969. "Das Begräbnis." In *Gruppe 47: Ein Querschnitt*, ed. Elizabeth Welt Trahan. Waltham, Mass.: Blaisdell, 3-10.

Clifford, James L. 1970. *From Portraits to Puzzles: Problems of a Literary Biographer*. Chapel Hill: University of North Carolina Press.

Gerber, Dieter. 1970. "Mary Stuart und ihr Bild heute." *General-Anzeiger* (Bonn), 23 December.

Esslin, Martin. 1971. *Brecht: The Man and His Work*. Garden City, N.Y.: Doubleday [1959].

Freedman, Ralph. 1971. *The Lyrical Novel: Studies in Hermann Hesse, André Gide and Virginia Woolf*. Princeton, N.J.: Princeton University Press [1963].

Jens, Walter. 1971a. (Untitled interview with Hildesheimer). In *Selbstanzeige: Schriftsteller im Gespräch*, ed. Werner Koch. Frankfurt am Main: Fischer, 89-99.

Rodewald, Dierk, ed. 1971a. *Über Wolfgang Hildesheimer*. Frankfurt am Main: Suhrkamp. Includes:
Baumgart, Reinhard. 1971. "Vor der Klagemauer." 115-18.
Ebert, Wolfgang.1971. "Abgegriffene Münzen." 94-95.
Heißenbüttel, Helmut. 1971. "Nur Erfindung, nur Täuschung?"118-21.
Jacobi, Johannes. 1971. "Hildesheimers Komödien." 96-98. Reprinted in Jehle 1989, 176-78.
Jens, Walter. 1971b. "Altväterliche Betrachtung." 81-83.
—. 1971c. "Ein Ausgelieferter übertönt die Nacht." 121-27.
Karasek, Hellmuth. 1971. "Ein Mann will schlafen." 111-14.
Karsch, Walter. 1971. "Zäher Spaß mit Wolfgang Hildesheimer." 100-2.
Koebner, Thomas. 1971. "Entfremdung und Melancholie: Zu Hildesheimers intellektuellen Helden." 32-59.
Morriën, Adriaan. 1971. "Die Satire kehrt in die deutsche Literatur zurück." 83-85.
Oellers, Norbert. 1971. "Bemerkungen über 'Mary Stuart.' Mit einigen Vorbemerkungen über das Verhältnis Autor-Publikum." 60-78.
Rodewald, Dierk. 1971b. "Wolfgang Hildesheimer im Gespräch mit Dierk Rodewald." 141-61.
Scheffer, Bernd. 1971. "Transposition und sprachlich erzeugte Situation: Zur dichterischen Verfahrensweise Wolfgang Hildesheimers." 17-31.
Schreiber, Ulrich. 1971. "Der schöne Tod auf der Bühne." 136-37.
Schwab-Felisch, Hans. 1971. "Mariechen auf dem Stein." 133-36.
Süskind, W. E. 1971. "Paradies der falschen Vögel." 86-87.
Wiegenstein, Roland H. 1971. "Nacht ohne Schlaf." 127-32.

Greif, Hans Jürgen. 1973. "Mary Stuart." In his *Zum modernen Drama: Martin Walser. Wolfgang Bauer. Rainer Werner Fassbinder. Siegfried Lenz. Wolfgang Hildesheimer*. Bonn: Bouvier, 76-88.

Hamburger, Käte. 1973. *The Logic of Literature*, trans. Marilynn J. Rose. Bloomington: Indiana University Press.

M. K. 1973. "Ovationen für das Gespann Becker/Freitag." *Schweinfurter Volkszeitung*, 12 February.

Neumann, Peter Horst. 1973. "Voreingenommene Bemerkungen: Zu Wolfgang Hildesheimers neuem Buch 'Masante'." *Merkur* 27: 494-97. Reprinted in Jehle 1989, 264-68.

Reich-Ranicki, Marcel. 1973. *Über Ruhestörer: Juden in der deutschen Literatur*. Munich: Piper.

Wapnewski, Peter. 1973. "Noch ein Aufbruch nach Tynset: Zu Wolfgang Hildesheimers neuem Buch 'Masante'." *Die neue Rundschau* 84: 324-27.

Zimmer, Dieter E. 1973. "Rückzug aus dem Leben."*Die Zeit,* 13 April.

Barthes, Roland. 1975. *The Pleasure of the Text*, trans. Richard Miller. New York: Hill and Wang.

Haas, Patricia R. 1975. "*Tynset*: An Analysis of Wolfgang Hildesheimer's lyrical modernism." Diss. University of Virginia.

Kurz, Paul Konrad. 1975. *Zwischen Entfremdung und Utopie: Die Neuentdeckung des Poetischen*. Frankfurt am Main: Knecht, 72-76.

Mann, Thomas. 1975. *Die Erzählungen*. Volume 1. Frankfurt am Main: Fischer Taschenbuch Verlag, 282-88.

Nef, Ernst. 1975. "Die absurde Geschichte; die Fälscher, die Häscher; der Melancholiker: Wolfgang Hildesheimers Weg von der absurden Geschichte zum subjektiven Erzähler." *Schweizer Monatshefte* 55: 37-45.

Petuchowski, Elizabeth Mayer. 1975. " 'Emptiness' and Related Images in Wolfgang Hildesheimer's *Tynset* and *Masante*." Diss. University of Cincinnati.

Derrida, Jacques. 1976. *Of Grammatology*, trans. Gayatri Chakravorty Spivak. Baltimore: Johns Hopkins University Press.

Dücker, Burckhard. 1976. *Wolfgang Hildesheimer und die deutsche Literatur des Absurden*. Bensberg-Frankenforst: Schäuble.

Durzak, Manfred. 1976. *Gespräche über den Roman*. Frankfurt am Main: Suhrkamp.

Hart-Nibbrig, Christiaan L. 1976. "Der andere Ton: Zur Musikalität von Wolfgang Hildesheimers Prosa." *Merkur* 30: 1201-7.

Hill, Linda M. 1976. *Language as Aggression: Studies in Postwar Drama*. Bonn: Bouvier.

Kerle, Heinz. 1976. ". . . für mich ist es jetzt mit der Fiktion vorbei." *Bündner Zeitung*, 9 December.

Watson, Donald. 1976. "Ionesco and His Early English Critics." In *Eugene Ionesco: Plays*. Volume 10, trans. Donald Watson. London: Calder, 115-34.

Foucault, Michel. 1977. "What Is an Author?" In *Language, Counter-Memory, Practice*, ed. Donald F. Bouchard. Ithaca, N.Y.: Cornell University Press, 113-38.

Stanley, Patricia Haas. 1977. "Verbal Music in Theory and Practice." *The Germanic Review* 52: 217-25. Reprinted in *Literature and Music: Essays in Form*, ed. Nancy Anne Cluck. Provo: Brigham Young University Press, 1981, 44-52.

Burroughs, William S., with Brion Gysin. 1978. *The Third Mind*. New York: Seaver.

Eykman, Christoph. 1978. "Erfunden oder Vor-Gefunden? Zur Integration des Außerfiktionalen in die epische Fiktion." *Neophilologus* 62: 319-34.

Hoyt, Giles. 1978. "Guilt in Absurdity: Wolfgang Hildesheimer's *Tynset*." *Seminar* 14: 133-40.

Puknus, Heinz. 1978. *Wolfgang Hildesheimer*. Munich: Beck.

Andersson, Björn. 1979. *Zur Gestaltung von Entfremdung bei Wolfgang Hildesheimer*. Stockholm: Almqvist & Wiksell.

Lea, Henry A. 1979. "Wolfgang Hildesheimer and the German-Jewish Experience." *Monatshefte* 71: 19-28.

Scheuer, Helmut. 1979. *Biographie: Studien zur Funktion und zum Wandel einer literarischen Gattung vom 18. Jahrhundert bis zur Gegenwart*. Stuttgart: Metzler.

Schmolze, Gerhard. 1979. "Mozart und die Religion." *Zeitwende: Die neue Furche* 50: 1-24.

Stanley, Patricia Haas. 1979a. "The Structure of Wolfgang Hildesheimer's *Tynset*." *Monatshefte* 71: 29-40.

—. 1979b. "Wolfgang Hildesheimer's *Mary Stuart*: Language Run Riot." *Germanic Review* 54: 110-14.

Wetzel, Heinz. 1979. "Namen in Hildesheimers *Masante*: 'Schall und Rauch' oder 'Schächte des Schreckens'?" *Seminar* 25: 143-62.

Faber, Marion. 1980. "Wolfgang Hildesheimer's *Mozart* as Meta-Biography." *biography* 3: 202-8.

Scher, Helene. 1980. "British Queens in German Drama: Elizabeth and Mary in plays by Schiller, Bruckner and Hildesheimer." In *Theatrum Mundi: Essays on German Drama and German Literature*, ed. Edward R. Haymes. Munich: Fink, 159-74.

Shaffer, Peter. 1980. *Amadeus*. New York: New American Library.

Stanley, Patricia Haas, trans. 1980. "The Absurd 'I'." *Denver Quarterly* 15.3: 92-105.

Zeller, Rosemarie. 1980. "Biographie und Roman." *Zeitschrift für Literaturwissenschaft und Linguistik* 40: 107-26.

Bergman, Rolf. 1981. "Eine Biographie über einen erfundenen Helden." *Mannheimer Morgen*, 9 December.

Heißenbüttel, Helmut. 1981. "Die Puppe in der Puppe, oder Der Hildesheimer im Marbot." *Süddeutsche Zeitung*, 21-22 November. Reprinted in Jehle 1989, 302-5.

Jens, Tismar. 1981. *Das deutsche Kunstmärchen des zwanzigsten Jahrhunderts*. Stuttgart: Metzler, 107-9.

Kaelin, Eugene. 1981. *The Unhappy Consciousness: The Poetic Plight of Samuel Beckett. An Inquiry at the Intersection of Phenomenology and Literature*. Dordrecht, Holland: Reidel.

Kleinstück, Johannes. 1981. "Sündiger englischer Aristokrat." *Die Welt*, 14 October.

Martinez-Bonati, Félix. 1981. *Fictive Discourse and the Structures of Literature: A Phenomenological Approach*, trans. Philip W. Silver. Ithaca: Cornell University Press.

Petrie, Dennis W.1981. *Ultimately Fiction*. W. Lafayette: Purdue University Press.

Ekonomu, Andrew J. 1982. Review of *Mozart*. *The Atlanta Journal/Constitution*, 7 November.

Jauß, Hans Robert. 1982. "Hildesheimers Reprise von Schillers *Maria Stuart.*" In his *Ästhetische Erfahrung und literarische Hermeneutik*. Frankfurt am Main: Suhrkamp, 797-806.

Kesting, Hanjo. 1982. "Im Spiegelkabinett der ästhetischen Existenz." *Frankfurter Rundschau*, 20 February.

Krättli, Anton. 1982. "Ein Gesprächspartner Goethes aus Wörtern. Wolfgang Hildesheimer: 'Marbot' – eine Biographie." *Schweizer Monatshefte* 2: 159-63.

Raddatz, Fritz. 1982. "Die Prosa Wolfgang Hildesheimers." *Die neue Rundschau* 93.4: 58-66.

Schabert, Ina. 1982. "Fictional Biography, Factual Biography and their Contaminations." *biography* 5: 1-16.

Stern, J. P. 1982. "Sweet Sin." *London Review of Books*, 5-18 August, 3-7.

Tyson, Alan. 1982. "Amadevious." *New York Times Book Review*, 18 November, 3-7.

Wapnewski, Peter. 1982. "Wie wahrscheinlich ist das Wahre?" *Der Spiegel*, 4 January, 109-112.

Craft, Robert. 1983. "New Legends for Old." *Atlantic*, 10 April, 130-32.

Fitzlyon, April. 1983. Review of *Marbot*. *Literary Review*, 21 November.

Foucault, Michel. 1983. *This Is Not a Pipe. With Illustrations and Letters by René Magritte*, trans. and ed. James Harkness. Berkeley: University of California Press.

Hefner, Arthur W. 1983. "Flushing out the story of Sir Andrew Marbot." *Boston Globe*, 4 September.

Porter, Peter. 1983. "The Mystery and the Music. On Mozart's Life." *Encounter*, June, 53-58.

Schiff, Gert. 1983. "Illusionäre Wunscherfüllung zu Wolfgang Hildesheimers Marbot." *Idea: Jahrbuch der Hamburger Kunsthalle 2. Kunst um 1800*, ed. Werner Hofmann und Martin Warnke. Hamburg: Prestel, 137-50. Reprinted in Jehle 1989, 307-22.

Simon, John. 1983. "A Passion for Art and Mother." *New York Times Book Review*, 9 October, 11-13.

Stanley, Patricia. 1983. "Wolfgang Hildesheimer's *Das Opfer Helena*: Another Triumph of the 'They.' " In *From Pen to Performance. Drama as Conceived and Performed*. 3, ed. Karelisa V. Hartigan. Lanham, Md.: University Press of America, 111-20.

Watt, Roderick. 1983. "Self-Defeating Satire? On the Function of the Implied Reader in Wolfgang Hildesheimer's *Lieblose Legenden*." *Forum for Modern Language Studies* 19: 58-74.

Weinhold, Ulrike. 1983. "Die Absurdität Wolfgang Hildesheimers." *Amsterdamer Beiträge zur neueren Germanistik* 16: 329-62.

Weisstein, Ulrich. 1983. "Wolfgang Hildesheimer's *Marbot*: Fictional Biography and Treatise on Comparative Literature." *Yearbook of Comparative and General Literature* 32: 23-38.

Affentranger, Angelika. 1984. "Ich bin ein grosser Pessimist. Wolfgang Hildesheimers 'Mitteilungen an Max....' " *Zürichsee-Zeitung*, 3 February.

Blau, Douglas. 1984. Review of *Marbot. Art in America*, February, 21.

Jehle, Volker. 1984. *Wolfgang Hildesheimer: Eine Bibliographie.* Frankfurt am Main: Lang.

Martin, George. 1984. *The Companion to Twentieth Century Opera.* New York: Dodd, Mead [1979].

Seemann, Hellmut. 1984. "Das Gesetz Sowohl-Als-Übel." *Deutsches Allgemeines Sonntagsblatt,* 26 February.

Blamberger, Günter. 1985. *Versuch über den deutschen Gegenwartsroman.* Stuttgart: Metzler, 74-100.

Hamburger, Käte. 1985. "Marbot – Eine Biographie." In *Romanistik Integrativ: Festschrift für Wolfgang Pollak,* ed. Wolfgang Bandhauer and Robert Tanzmeister. Vienna: Braumüller, 195-204.

Rath, Wolfgang. 1985. *Fremd im Fremden: Zur Scheidung von Ich und Welt im deutschen Gegenwartsroman.* Heidelberg: Winter, 79-161.

Riehn, Rainer. 1985. "Die Zauberflöte: Machwerk = Werk-Stück/Stück-Werk = Lehr-Stück, oder Mozart, der dialektische Komponist." In *Musik-Konzepte 3. Mozart. Ist die Zauberflöte ein Machwerk?* ed. Heinz-Klaus Metzger and Rainer Riehn. Munich: Vollendorf, 34-68.

Schneider, Thomas. 1985. "Die Antwort als Klopfzeichen." *Text & Kontext* 13.2: 355-81.

Umbach, Klaus. 1985. " Amadeus – das Ferkel, das Feuer speit." *Der Spiegel,* 16 September, 238-51.

Arens, Katherine. 1986. "Mozart: A Case Study of Logocentric Repression." *Comparative Literature Studies* 23: 141-69.

Arnold, Heinz Ludwig, ed. 1986. *Text + Kritik 89/90: Wolfgang Hildesheimer.* Munich: edition text+kritik. Includes:
Blamberger, Günter. 1986. "Der Rest ist Schweigen." 33-44.
Bormann, Alexander von. 1986. "Der Skandal einer perfekten Biographie: Über 'Marbot. Eine Biographie.' " 69-82.
Jens, Walter. 1986. "Wolfgang Hildesheimer: ein bildender Künstler." 1-7.
Kesting, Hanjo. 1986. " 'Mozart' und 'Marbot' – Spiegelbilder? Ein Gespräch." 83-89.

Lauffs, Manfred. 1986. "Reden ist Gold: 'Die Eroberung der Prinzessin Turandot' als politische Satire und poetologische Parabel." 103-7.

Loquai, Franz. 1986. "Auf der Suche nach Weite: Zur Prosa Wolfgang Hildesheimer." 45-62.

Lorenz, Christoph F. 1986. "Das fragende Theater des Wolfgang Hildesheimer." 90-102.

Neumann, Peter Horst. 1986. "Hildesheimers Ziel und Ende: Über 'Marbot' und die Folgerichtigkeit des Gesamtwerks." 20-32.

Puknus, Heinz. 1986. "Das Scheitern der Welt: Hildesheimers Hörspiele der siebziger Jahre." 106-16.

Weerdenburg, Oscar van. 1986. "Hildesheimers Mozartbuch." 63-68.

Beck, Hans-Joachim. 1986. *Der Selbstmord als eine schöne Kunst begangen: Prolegomena zu Wolfgang Hildesheimers psychoanalytischem Roman 'Marbot.'* Frankfurt am Main: Lang.

Brater, Enoch, ed. 1986. *Beckett at 80. Beckett in Context..* New York: Oxford University Press. Includes:
Beckerman, Bernard. 1986. "Beckett and the Act of Listening." 149-67.
Esslin, Martin. 1986. "Samuel Beckett – Infinity, Eternity." 110-23.

McClymonds, Marita P. 1986. Review of *Mozart. The Eighteenth Century: A Current Bibliography. n.s.* 8 – *for* 1982, ed. Jim Springer Borck. 4. New York: A M S Press, 277-78.

Richter, Hans Werner. 1986. *Im Etablissement der Schmetterlinge. Einundzwanzig Portraits aus der Gruppe 47.* Munich: Hanser, 138-48.

Baumgart, Reinhard. 1987. "Stoßseufzer der Sprache." *Die Zeit,* 10 July.

Hart-Nibbrig, Christiaan L. 1987. "Flucht-Trotz. Eine Collage aus und mit und über Wolfgang Hildesheimers Ästhetik des Zwischenraums." *Die neue Rundschau* 98.2: 82-99. Reprinted in Jehle 1989, 89-113.

Neugroschel, Joachim, trans. 1987. *The Collected Stories of Wolfgang Hildesheimer.* New York: The Ecco Press.

Petuchowski, Elizabeth Mayer. 1987. "Typically Hildesheimer: A German Adaptation of Richard Brinsley Sheridan's *The School for Scandal.*" In *Exile and Enlightenment: Studies in German and Comparative Literature in Honor of Guy Stern*, ed. U w e Faulhaber et al. Detroit: Wayne State University Press, 257-63.

Postma, Heiko. 1987. "Ich trage eine Eule nach Athen." *Die Horen* 32.1: 215-22.

Reichert, Klaus. 1987. "Aus der Fremde und zurück." *Die neue Rundschau* 98.2: 67-81.

Silberman, Marc. 1987. "Writing What – for Whom? *Vergangen heitsbewältigung* in GDR Literature." *German Studies Review* 10: 527-38.

Jehle, Volker. 1988. "Nachwort." In *Wolfgang Hildesheimer: Die Hörspiele*, ed. Volker Jehle. Frankfurt am Main: Suhrkamp, 437-56.

Stanley, Patricia H. 1988. *The Realm of Possibilities: Wolfgang Hildesheimer's Non-Traditional Non-Fictional Prose.* Lanham, Md.: University Press of America.

Zimmermann, Bernhard. 1988. "Literary Criticism from 1933 to the Present." In *A History of German Literary Criticism, 1730-1980*, ed. Peter Uwe Hohendahl. Lincoln: University of Nebraska Press, 359-437.

Goll-Bickmann, Dietmar. 1989. *Aspekte der Melancholie in der frühen und mittleren Prosa Wolfgang Hildesheimers.* Münster: Lit.

Hanenberg, Peter. 1989. *Geschichte im Werk Wolfgang Hildesheimers.* Frankfurt am Main: Lang.

Jehle, Volker, ed. 1989. *Wolfgang Hildesheimer.* Frankfurt am Main: Suhrkamp. Includes:
Baumgart, Reinhard. 1989. "Heimisch im Absurden." 339-43.
Böll, Heinrich. 1989. "Ironisierter Kulturbetrieb." 165-66.
Fest, Joachim. 1989. "Mozart – das diskrete Genie." 289-94
Hartlaub, Geno. 1989. "Endstation Meona." 261-63.
Heißenbüttel, Helmut. 1989. "Die Puppe in der Puppe oder Der Hildesheimer im Marbot." 302-5.
Herzog, Valentin. 1989. "Der älteste Alptraum." 279-80.

Hochkeppel, Willy. 1989. "Ja, ich trinke, Du auch?" 324-27.

Jens, Tilman. 1989. "Über das Fremdsein." 336-38.

Jens, Walter. 1989. "Spiele, die einen Literaten begeistern." 172-75.

Kaiser, Joachim. 1989. "Mozart, das Ungeheuer." 284-88.

Krolow, Karl. 1989. "Mit Anmut modern." 156.

Lea, Henry A. 1989. "Hildesheimers Weg zum Ende der Fiktionen." 45-57.

Lenz, Hermann. 1989. "Das unbekannte Ziel." 190-91.

Muschg, Adolf. 1989. "Kein Mozart zum Anfassen." 295-300.

Neumann, Peter Horst. 1989. "Hamlet will schlafen." 205-11.

Petuchowski, Elizabeth Mayer. 1989. "Ein Hörspiel mit vielen Facetten." 276-77.

Piontek, Heinz. 1989. "Heitere Spiegelbilder." 163-64.

Plessen, Elisabeth. 1989. "Fuchs in Cornwall." 250-56.

Reich-Ranicki, Marcel. 1989. "Leider kein Striptease." 244-48.

Weiss, Peter. 1989. Letter to Hildesheimer, 27 December 1978. 282-83.

Wellershoff, Dieter. 1989. "Land der Fälscher." 160-62.

Westphal, Gert. 1989. "Der Regisseur zu seinem Autor." 168-70.

Wohmann, Gabriele. 1989. "Nachtmonolog." 202-4.

Meyer, Martin. 1989. "Leere Welt: Wolfgang Hildesheimers 'Vergebliche Aufzeichnungen.' " *Neue Zürcher Zeitung*, 26 January.

Schaeffer, Jean-Marie. 1989. "Loup, si on jouait au loup? (Feinte, simulacre et art)." *Autrement dire* 6: 111-123.

Schalk, Axel. 1989. *Geschichtsmaschinen: Über dem Umgang mit Historie in der Dramatik des technischen Zeitalters*. Heidelberg: Winter, 125-37.

Selden, Raman. 1989. *A Reader's Guide to Contemporary Literary Theory*. Lexington: University of Kentucky Press.

"Spiegel Gespräch." 1989. *Der Spiegel*, 2 January, 140-46.

Cohn, Dorrit. 1990. "Signposts of Fictionality: A Narratological Perspective." *Poetics Today* 11: 775-804.

Hartje, Hans. 1990. "Wolfgang Hildesheimer. L'Art sert à inventer la vérité." *littérature* 77.2: 75-78.

Japp, Uwe. 1990. "Das Ende der Kunst des Schreibens: Wolfgang Hildesheimer und 'Marbot.' " *Schriftenreihe der Universität Regensburg* 17, 211-26.

Jehle, Volker. 1990. *Wolfgang Hildesheimer: Werkgeschichte.* Frankfurt am Main: Suhrkamp.

Lebert, Stephan. 1990. "Verstummen, um die Welt zu verlieren." *Süddeutsche Zeitung*, 27/28 January.

Hart Nibbrig, Christiaan Lucas and Volker Jehle, eds. 1991. *Wolfgang Hildesheimer: Gesammelte Werke in sieben Bänden.* Frankfurt am Main: Suhrkamp

Michaelis, Rolf. 1991. "Endlich allein. Zum Tod von Wolfgang Hildesheimer." *Die Zeit*, 6 September.

Neumann, Peter Horst. 1991. "Hildesheimer als bildender Künstler." In *Wolfgang Hildesheimer: Rede an die Jugend.* Weilheimer Hefte zur Literatur 31. Weilheim: Gymnasium Weilheim, n.p.

Seiler, Manfred. 1991. "Wie man als Meister vom Himmel fällt." *Die Zeit*, 18 October.

Cohn, Dorrit. 1992. "Breaking the Code of Fictional Biography: Wolfgang Hildesheimer's *Marbot.*" In *Traditions of Experiment from the Enlightenment to the Present: Essays in Honor of Peter Demetz*, ed. Nancy Kaiser and David E. Wellbery. Ann Arbor: University of Michigan Press, 301-19.

Zorach, Cecile Cazort. 1992. "Peter Handke as Translator of Walker Percy." *South Atlantic Review* 57: 69-87.

Stanley, Patricia. 1994. "Sum, ergo spero? Wolfgang Hildesheimer's Tentative Absurd Hope." *Seminar.*

Index

Adamov, Arthur 2
Adams, Timothy Dow 70
Adorno, Theodor 95
Affentranger, Angelika 85, 130
Aichinger, Ilse 31
Allen, Woody 74
Altick, Richard D. 51, 123
Andersson, Djörn 3, 4, 15, 24-27, 37, 41,
    85, 87, 93-95, 97-99, 108, 127
Arens, Katherine 35, 54, 57, 58, 61,
    103, 104, 131
Aristotle 72
Arnold, Heinz Ludwig 78, 13
Arrabal, Fernando 94
Aue, Hartmann von 66

Baer, Volker 96, 123
Baltrusch, Peter 122
Barnes, Djuna 10, 31, 95, 112, 118-120,
    123
Barthes, Roland 66, 126
Baudelaire, Charles Pierre 56
Baumgart, Reinhard 18, 19, 77, 108,
    110, 125, 132, 133
Beck, Hans-Joachim 52, 63, 65-68, 70,
    72, 74, 77, 116, 132
Becker, Jürgen 75, 76
Beckerman, Bernard 84, 94, 132
Beckett, Samuel 2, 9, 25, 29, 31, 32, 49,
    80, 84, 89, 94, 95, 97, 101, 112
Beethoven, Ludwig van 10, 53
Bellow, Saul 74
Bergman, Rolf 62, 128
Bernhard, Thomas 24
Blamberger, Günter 5, 15, 24, 26-29,
    38, 39, 42, 43, 71, 85, 108, 109, 116,
    131
Blau, Douglas 63, 70, 130
Blöcker, Günter 9, 10, 123
Böll, Heinrich 11, 20, 24, 58, 82, 133
Borchert, Wolfgang 79
Borges, Jorge Luis 9, 10, 31
Bormann, Alexander von 66, 72, 131
Boswell, James 6, 67
Brater, Enoch 132

Brecht, Bertolt 55, 88, 93
Broch, Hermann 73
Büchner, Georg 18, 103
Burroughs, William S. 42, 127
Byron, George Gordon (called Lord)
    66

Camus, Albert 3, 9, 31, 86, 89, 90, 103
Cervantes, Miguel de 32
Chapman, Frederick Spencer 112, 118
Clifford, James L. 6, 124
Cohn, Dorrit 61, 64, 69, 73, 74, 116,
    134, 135
Congreve, William 80, 105, 122
Courts, Gerd 123
Craft, Robert 53, 57, 58, 129

da Vinci, Leonardo 10
de Bruyn, Günter 52
Derrida, Jacques 52, 126
Döblin, Alfred 17, 36
Doctorow, E. L. 63
Dollfuß, Engelbert 37
Domin, Hilde 19, 22, 123
Dücker, Burckhard 2-4, 9, 14, 17, 24,
    25, 27, 31, 34, 43, 46, 49, 50, 74, 83,
    85, 87, 92, 94, 95, 97, 99, 101, 102,
    104, 108, 109, 116, 126
Dürrenmatt, Friedrich 81, 82
Durzak, Manfred 9, 11, 21, 26, 27, 31,
    32, 35, 42, 46, 60, 67, 115, 126

Ebert, Wolfgang 91, 125
Ehrig, Heinz 95
Eich, Günter 32, 44, 75, 82, 91
Ekonomu, Andrew J. 58, 129
Ellmann, Richard 56, 61
Emig, Erik 123
Enzensberger, Hans Magnus 52, 61
Esslin, Martin 3, 88, 89, 92, 102, 124,
    132
Eykman, Christoph 36, 66, 127

Faber, Marion 54, 55, 103, 128
Fest, Joachim 57, 133

Fitzlyon, April 63, 129
Flaubert, Gustav 56
Foucault, Michel 10, 47, 52, 88, 127, 130
Freedman, Ralph 30, 124
Freud Sigmund 66
Frisch, Max 24, 51, 75, 76, 81, 82

Gatter, Ludwig 87, 89, 122
Genet, Jean 2, 56
George, Stefan 77, 112
Gerber, Dieter 101, 124
Gide, André 30
Goebbels, Paul Joseph 37
Goeppert, Sebastian 58, 59
Goethe, August von 67
Goethe, Johann Wolfgang von 8, 54, 63, 66, 67, 68
Goldoni, Carlo 80, 105
Goldschmidt, Rudolf 91, 122
Goll-Bickmann, Dietmar 4-6, 11, 15-17, 21, 23, 24, 25, 27, 30, 41-43, 45, 47, 50, 51, 61, 99, 133
Gorey, Edward 112, 113, 118-120
Gozzi, Carlo 88
Grabbe, Christian Dietrich 103
Grass, Günter xii, 24, 58, 80
Greco, El (Domenico Theotocopoulos) 10
Greif, Hans Jürgen 103, 125
Gruber, Gernot 61
Guiscard, Robert 10
Gundermann, Max 82
Gysin, Brion 42, 127

Haas, Patricia R. 9, 20, 22-24, 27, 30, 62, 108, 116, 126
Hamburger, Käte 68, 73, 74, 115, 116, 125, 131
Handke, Peter 24, 114
Hanenberg, Peter 4, 5, 10, 11, 16, 17, 29-31, 36, 39, 40, 49, 51, 52, 54, 57, 58, 61, 71, 76, 82-90, 95, 96, 98, 100, 101, 103, 107, 133
Hart-Nibbrig, Christiaan Lucas 23, 24, 62, 90, 116, 127, 132
Hartje, Hans 74, 134
Hartlaub, Geno 32, 35, 42, 133
Hefner, Arthur W. 63, 130
Hegel, G. F. W. 72
Heidegger, Martin 34
Heidsieck, Arnold 27, 82, 94, 95, 124

Heißenbüttel, Helmut 19, 64, 67-69, 125, 128, 133
Henze, Hans Werner 87
Herzog, Valentin 86, 133
Hesse, Hermann xii, 30
Hill, Linda M. 10, 84, 91, 92, 93, 95-97, 100, 104, 116, 127
Hochhuth, Rolf 31, 100, 101, 107
Hochkeppel, Willy 74, 131, 134
Hoerschelmann, Fred von 82
Hofmannsthal, Hugo von 77
Hölderlin, Friedrich 4, 123
Homer 43
Hoyt, Giles 22-24, 39, 127

Ionesco, Eugene 2, 3, 10, 29, 31, 80-82, 89, 91, 94, 95, 97, 105, 109, 123

Jacobi, Johannes 91, 96, 125
Japp, Uwe 69, 71, 72, 73, 135
Jehle, Volker xii, xiii, 4, 6-9, 11, 12, 16, 17, 30, 32, 41, 42, 44, 46-48, 50,-54, 56, 59-66, 69, 72, 73, 75-77, 80-91, 95-97, 99, 101, 104-110, 112-116, 121, 122, 125, 126, 128, 130-133, 135
Jens, Tilman 68, 108, 134
Jens, Tismar 128
Jens, Walter 2, 10, 11, 18, 31, 32, 77, 104, 125, 131, 134
Johnson, Samuel 6, 67
Johnson, Uwe 24
Joyce, James xiii, 9, 31, 112, 113

Kaelin, Eugene 31, 128
Kafka, Franz xii, 32, 35, 36, 112
Kähler, Hermann 18, 19, 25, 27, 31, 124
Kaiser, Joachim 57, 134
Kandinsky, Wassily 65, 67
Karasek, Hellmuth 101, 125
Karsch, Walter 91, 125
Kayser, Wolfgang 94
Kerle, Heinz 52, 127
Kesting, Hanjo 52, 63, 64, 68, 69, 129, 131
Kleinstück, Johannes 63, 128
Kluge, Alexander 36
Koebner, Thomas 9, 14, 20, 21, 30, 42, 49, 92, 95-99, 125
Koeppen, Wolfgang 24
Krättli, Anton 62, 129
Krolow, Karl 2, 134

Kuiper, Pieter C. 58, 59
Kurz, Paul Konrad 33, 34, 43, 126

Lauffs, Manfred 88, 132
Lea, Henry A. 27-31, 37, 38, 43, 49, 93, 105, 127, 134
Leisegang, Herbert 123
Lenz, Hermann 15, 134
Loquai, Franz 9, 132
Lorenz, Christoph F. 88, 89, 98, 99, 132
Lubbock, Percy 65, 115, 124
Luft, Friedrich 91, 123

M. K. 101, 125
Magritte, René 88
Mailer, Norman 56
Manet, Edouard 36
Mann, Thomas xi, 8, 18, 19, 54, 66, 67, 74, 124, 126
Martinez-Bonati, Félix 116, 129
McClymonds, Marita P. 53, 132
Meckel, Christoph xii
Meyer, Frank A. 61
Meyer, Martin 18, 134
Michaelis, Rolf 117, 135
Middlebrook, Diane Wood 6
Monroe, Marilyn 44
Montaigne, Michel de 9, 107
Mörike, Eduard 57
Morriën, Adriaan 1, 11, 82, 125
Mozart, Wolfgang Amadeus xi, 35, 52-61, 73, 103, 104, 106, 107, 110
Muschg, Adolf 52, 62, 134

Nabokov, Vladimir xi, 74
Nef, Ernst 2, 4, 9, 10, 24, 34, 42, 126
Neugroschel, Joachim xi, xii, 74, 132
Neumann, Peter Horst xiii, 18, 32, 42, 52, 58, 71, 77, 85, 109, 116, 126, 132, 134, 135
Nietzsche, Friedrich 66, 72, 124
Nöhbauer, Hans F. 14, 123
Novalis (Friedrich Leopold Freiherr von Hardenberg) 66

Oellers, Norbert 102, 125

Percy, Walker 114
Petrie, Dennis W. 56, 129
Petuchowski, Elizabeth Mayer 20, 21, 27, 29, 30, 33, 43, 85, 86, 106, 126, 133, 134

Piontek, Heinz 11, 46, 134
Piper, Anne 112, 118, 119, 121
Plessen, Elisabeth 46, 49, 134
Porter, Peter 130
Postma, Heiko 67, 133
Puccini, Giacomo 88
Puknus, Heinz 2, 4, 8, 11, 15, 22, 25, 35, 36, 43, 48, 54, 82, 83, 85, 86, 88, 89, 99, 102, 127, 132

Raddatz, Fritz 62, 64, 68, 129
Rath, Wolfgang 21, 23, 24, 30, 31, 38, 40, 42, 43, 50, 131
Reich-Ranicki, Marcel 28, 45-50, 115, 126, 134
Reichert, Klaus 4, 5, 15, 24, 33, 43, 133
Richter, Hans Werner 1, 12, 28, 132
Riehn, Rainer 53, 131
Rilke, Rainer Maria 14, 77
Rischbieter, Henning 97, 123
Rodewald, Dierk 16, 32, 46-48, 51, 96, 102, 125

Sartre, Jean-Paul 56, 61, 89
Schabert, Ina 56, 61, 129
Schaeffer, Jean-Marie 73, 134
Schalk, Axel 103, 134
Scheffer, Bernd 84, 125
Scher, Helene 103, 128
Scheuer, Helmut 54, 127
Schiff, Gert 65, 67, 69, 116, 130
Schiller, Friedrich 54, 88, 101, 103
Schlegel, Friedrich 72
Schmolze, Gerhard 55, 128
Schneider, Thomas 75-77, 131
Schnurre, Wolfdietrich 11, 12, 124
Schopenhauer, Arthur 66
Schreiber, Ulrich 101, 125
Schulz, Uwe 124
Schwab-Felisch, Hans 18, 101, 102, 124, 125
Schwitzke, Heinz 79, 81, 82, 123
Searle, Ronald 112, 118
Seiler, Manfred 113, 135
Selden, Raman 134
Sendak, Maurice 107
Sexton, Anne 6
Shaffer, Peter 55, 57, 128
Shakespeare, William 5, 6, 17
Shaw, George Bernard 113, 114, 119, 120
Sheridan, Richard Brinsley 80, 105, 106, 119

Sieburg, Friedrich 2, 9
Silberman, Marc 49, 133
Simon, John 63, 130
Simonov, Konstantin 18
Sontag, Susan xi, 74
Stanley, Patricia H. 34, 43, 52-58, 60-62, 64, 65, 69-71, 73, 76, 77, 83, 85, 102-104, 116, 127, 128, 130, 133, 135
Stern, J. P. 63, 129
Süskind, W. E. 11, 91, 122, 125
Swinarski, Konrad 101

Taëni, Rainer 95
Tyson, Alan 53, 129

Umbach, Klaus 55, 131

Vielhaber, Gerd 123

Wagner, Richard 66
Walser, Martin 24
Wapnewski, Peter 32, 36, 43, 50, 63, 64, 77, 126, 129
Watson, Donald 123, 127
Watt, Roderick 4, 7, 8, 36, 130
Watteau, Antoine 8
Weber, Carl Maria von 10

Weerdenburg, Oscar van 54, 58, 59, 61, 132
Weinhold, Ulrike 94, 95, 97-101, 103, 109, 110, 130
Weiss, Peter xii, 62, 134
Weisstein, Ulrich 65, 67-69, 72, 73, 77, 116, 130
Wellershoff, Dieter 11, 134
Westphal, Gert 105, 134
Wetzel, Heinz 36, 37, 40, 41, 43, 85, 128
Wiegenstein, Roland H. 18, 19, 95, 125
Wiesel, Elie 31
Wilde, Oscar 10, 105
Wimberger, Gerhard 89
Wisse, Jan 86
Wittgenstein, Ludwig 48, 51, 52
Wohmann, Gabrielle 10, 18, 134
Wolf, Christa xi, 18, 50, 52
Woolf, Virginia 30, 31, 70

Zeller, Rosemarie 54, 128
Zimmer, Dieter E. 60, 67, 77, 126
Zimmermann, Bernhard 2, 9, 46, 133
Zorach, Cecile Cazort 114, 135